IN THE CELLAR

IN THE CELLAR

Jan Philipp Reemtsma

Translated by Carol Brown Janeway

 Alfred A. Knopf   New York   1999

THIS IS A BORZOI BOOK
PUBLISHED BY ALFRED A. KNOPF, INC.

Originally published in Germany as *Im Keller*
by Hamburger Edition, Hamburg, in 1997.
Copyright © 1997 by Hamburger Edition

Library of Congress Cataloging-in-Publication Data
Reemtsma, Jan Philipp.
[Im Keller. English]
In the cellar / by Jan Philipp Reemtsma ; translated
by Carol Brown Janeway. — 1st American ed.
　　　　　　　　　　p.　　cm.
ISBN 0-375-40098-2 (hc)
1. Reemtsma, Jan Philipp—Kidnapping, 1996. 2. Kid-
napping—Germany—Case studies.　I. Title.
HV6604.G42R4413　1999
364.15'4'092—dc21
[B]　　98-35256　　CIP

Manufactured in the United States of America
First American Edition

For all those to whom we owe thanks

IN THE CELLAR

I had actually wanted to come home. Midnight; first the wood where they turned me loose, then the village and the first house where lights were still burning, and the man who lived there let me in without any ifs and buts, though I must have seemed like some weird tramp to him. I called my wife, said, "It's me. I'm free." And I wanted to call for a taxi, go home, just like that, only three quarters of an hour, you can manage that. And then the moment, thirty-three days of longing, although for these thirty-three days I had forbidden myself to imagine it: I'm standing at the front door, I ring, my wife opens the door, and now, now I could—what? Weep, probably, perhaps just fall over, no, not quite, but suddenly become a great weight in my wife's arms, unable to bear the tension by myself for another second, and then (or have I done that already?) hold her tight, absorb her stress . . . no, we would go up to our son (or has he heard me and is he on his way downstairs?), and all three of us are by his bed (or sitting on the carpet) holding each other close.

"I—I'll call a taxi and I'll be there in three quarters of an hour." I said something along those lines, thereby demonstrating that my four and a half weeks in the cellar had cost me all sense of reality. She said she wanted to come and get me and "We're flying to New York." But I wanted to go home. A moment's confusion. Then my mind starts working again: I have no idea what's going on out there, I've lost touch, it's her decision.

For the next half hour I tell my host a scrambled version of what has happened to me. Then the police are there, and my wife is with them. No—no hugging. First all my clothes into these plastic bags to preserve any traces of evidence. We go into an adjoining room. I undress, notice once again how unsteady I am on my feet. Then we embrace. My host for the evening said later during a TV interview that the feeling we transmitted to him was "relief"—and instead of the German word, he used the English *relief,* with its echo of a breath released at last—and he was right.

Next, the trip to the hospital. A fairly thorough examination by a woman doctor on night call who has been wakened, but not told anything about the circumstances, who learned from me that I had been held captive for weeks in a cellar, and who took it as a sign of my disorientation that I couldn't immediately come up with the exact date of my abduction (was it the twenty-fifth or the twenty-seventh?). The fact that she wrote in her case notes that she didn't know whether a special psychological examination was indicated or not was a sign of her uncertainty and doubtless the right thing to do. I seemed to be in better shape than I actually felt, and in much worse shape than I believed.

My balance wasn't very good, I was talking quickly, my words tumbling over each other at manic speed, I wanted to give my account, be free of it, able to do something at long last, say something, be able to contribute something so that we could find the people who had done this to me.

In the meantime, a police car had brought my son to the hospital. They told me he'd arrived; he came hesitantly into the room where I'd been giving my statement to the police. As I only discovered later, he'd given up believing he would ever see me alive again. A hug, as tender as could be, as matter-of-factly father-son as necessary. A glance at my beard, since there had been no razor in the cellar. My son was truly getting an unknown father back.

Shower. Wash hair. Look in the mirror, the first time for four and a half weeks. We all shared a room in the hospital. No one could sleep. "When did you notice that I was gone?" "What went wrong at the handover?" A chaos of fragments of information, in which my own memory of thirty-three days chained in a cellar threatens to drown. Names I don't recognize. Police who have spent almost all this time living in our house, sharing its routine, sleeping camped out under the table, taking my son on excursions, helping my wife. Bottomless gratitude. In the cellar I had never been able to picture how it was at home, never wanted to, either. Now I know that there were people to help.

Police. Relatives. Friends. They weren't on their own.

I don't have much to tell. This, that. This is how it looked. That's how long the chain was. Food? Mostly bread and cold cuts. Yes, I'm having trouble walking, because of inflamed tendons in both feet as a result of pacing to and fro with chains on. Yes, and my right thumb is completely numb, as a result of the badly fastened handcuffs from four and a half weeks ago. No, I didn't tell the doctor, what's the point, that's the least of my problems.

So why are we flying to New York? Do I have any idea how it looks "at home"? As if Greta Garbo had come for a visit. The first time it becomes really clear to me is when we're back again after eight days away and I cautiously view the videotapes of the TV coverage. The very idea that I could have just come home by taxi was absurd, to say the least. Assault waves of flashing cameras, outstretched microphones, the usual barrage of questions along the standard lines of "How do you feel, Herr Reemtsma?" "Do you have any idea who is behind this?" and so on. You don't go home, you go on television. I had the means, the good luck, and the money to get away from them (a clever camera team, following up on a tip from God knows where, filmed us by telephoto lens as we were getting into the plane). For anyone without such resources, it can be pretty bad.

I'm in no way talking just about myself. Newspapers worldwide print the photo of the little Belgian girl Sabine Dardenne, freed after months of being held hostage, during which time she was tortured and filmed in the process. She was released, and her face shows no sign of relief, only horror and despair. Behind her is an embarrassed policeman who, as luck would have it, is holding the girl as if he were trying to restrain her so that she can be caught by the photographer. The photographer is no accident. Now she's going to be captured on film all over again.

The press loves to talk about the right to freedom of information. What kind of information is the face of a weeping, desperate, raped girl? And even if it were "information," how does that right compare with Sabine Dardenne's right not to be put on film? This is an extreme case, admittedly, but newspapers are in the business of extreme cases, that's what makes up their editions.

I cannot complain. In my case, the media kept silent for four weeks. Some weeks later there was another such case, one which ran its course differently and came to a different end. A man was enticed into a cinema, murdered, the family was blackmailed by his killers for a week before the police were able to arrest them. This time the silence of the press—unbeknownst to anyone—could achieve nothing to preserve the life of the supposed hostage, but perhaps it was of some help to the police in their work.

After four and a half weeks of silence, there was an immense need on the part of the media not just to take the information which they had freely been given—albeit with urgent pleas to publish it only after my release or my death, and in any case only with the consent of the police—and turn it into articles, priority broadcasts, specials, and who knows what else, but also to enter the usual race and come up with something that the competition didn't have. I read in the paper that I play golf with a well-known lady from Hamburg, even though I have never laid hands on a golf club. Helicopters took aerial photographs of our property, and later a photographer wrote to me asking me to let him get on with his job, because it was already the weekend and he wanted to get to his girlfriend in Itzehoe.

These are the attendant comedies. The feeling they evoke is one of an unending attempted assault. This can't be blamed on the behavior of the individual members of the press—they are often perfectly nice, and somehow you have the sense that certain aspects of their profession cause them some embarrassment— but simply on their incessant presence. For hour upon hour you lead a life in which these people whom you don't know, with whom you have nothing to do, and who are merely being paid to have something to do with you, have a role to play which cannot be ignored, and have to be included in all your plans. If you don't want someone taking photographs in through your windows (and you don't), you have to close the curtains. If you want to go to the mailbox without giving an interview (and you have nothing to say, and all you want to do is go to the mailbox), you have to send someone ahead of you to check if the street is empty, and if it isn't, you stay inside your home—which of course is no longer your home but a hiding place that you have to seal tight against trespassing eyes.

At some point I gave up. I was given the news that they would withdraw if I agreed to show myself. I went outside the door, let the ones who were there take their photographs, and okay. Word got around. A few hours later the next team of photographers and cameramen arrived, wearing expressions that said, "Why not us?" And in the mail the next day a threat from a laggard newspaper, to the effect that if they were not given the same treatment, they would have to try other measures. The best thing to do was to wait it out; the public was soon so saturated with items about Reemtsma that everyone lost interest. Other headlines soon came to dominate public attention, and all cameras were turned on Lower Saxony.

It was all a burden, sometimes worse than a burden, but it could have been still worse. A staffer on a news magazine who caught me (the street had seemed so empty of observers) even apologized for disturbing me, and then again even more wholeheartedly when I called his attention to the reporting in his paper— "About one sentence in two was accurate"—"Please forgive us, I'm really sorry, but our editorial offices are not in Hamburg!" Good advice came from our lawyer to give a major interview to one newspaper—and not one of the Hamburg ones but one that had space for a long conversation (we chose the *Süddeutsche Zeitung,* in Munich, which was also a way of saying a private thank-you)—and then refer everyone else to this. The *Süddeutsche* sold reprint rights all over the place, so everyone got something out of it.

The pictures and film clips of me outside my front door ran daily, whether they fit the latest news or not. "No new developments in Reemtsma case." Photo. "The Hamburg multimillionaire was abducted from in front of his house in Blankenese on March 25 and freed after payment of a $20 million ransom. It is thought that . . ." And then some piece of irrelevance that uses up so much text that the entire filmstrip can be reused. One of many letters of advice ("In future, get a Doberman") reached me, this one focused on the press: "You should not be in the press all the time. It will only make your face well known, and other criminals will come after you!" Thank you very much.

There was yet another photo. My abductors had snapped it in the cellar to which they had taken me. I am sitting in the jogging suit they gave me to wear there, my eyes are closed and I'm on a chair, with a table at an angle behind me on which a few utensils are scattered. I am holding the *Bild Zeitung* of March 26 up in front of me so that the headline and date are visible, and next to me is the silhouette of a man pointing a Kalashnikov at me. The whole thing is some kind of direct quote from previous abductions, the Kalashnikov in the ensemble lifted straight from the emblem of the Red Army Faction. The face in the photograph is swollen, the nose most of all, and there's a gash on the forehead. My wife had given instructions that the photograph was not to be used. After my release, the police asked permission to release it, retouched, to aid their investigations. It was published accordingly with the face blanked out, because the picture also contained a partial view of the cellar. My wife wanted to ensure a sliver of privacy in the general media frenzy, and to protect me from having my own beaten face be the first thing I saw when I opened the newspaper. These wise precautions were immediately ignored. Both *Bild* and *Stern* got hold of illegal copies of the photograph, recolored all the areas they felt were inadequate in the Polaroid, and printed the image in maximum enlargement. Oddly enough, given that I have spent a lifetime avoiding having my picture in the papers, this didn't bother me too much. I was amazed at my own indifference. It was a mixture of "It's completely irrelevant now" and "That's not me anyway"— to me the face in the cellar was a document from somebody else's life. Except that this wasn't true. Just how untrue became clear to me when I was invited by Grüner & Jahr, the publishers of *Stern* magazine, to give a short address about the press coverage of my "case" at the public awards ceremony for a prize they were giving in journalism. This bizarre request for yet another act of self-exhibition was a sudden and unpleasant revelation to me of how appalling the first had been: to present my face to the public just as the abductors had presented it to my wife.

So why once again? Why show my face in this book yet again, this time in words, this time of my own accord? This time, precisely because of all that, *because* it's all already in the public domain, because my story is already common currency, because it became public property within hours after my release, so that what I want is not only to reclaim it for myself (which is why I began *immediately* after my release to write all this down) but also to reclaim it *in public*. It is an extraordinary experience to see one's own life decompose into "stories" which are retailed to the public in versions cut to fit each medium. There is no copyright on your own life, but it is easier to come to terms with every kind of misappropriation of it if there is a standing text somewhere to which you can point.

Another thought from a completely different quarter is also relevant here. I learned that it was helpful to know the details of other abductions. To know a little bit about what it's like for others in moments of fear, of feeling lost, of worrying about those who are worrying about you. I received letters from people who had either experienced themselves, or had relatives who had experienced, something similar, indeed often much worse, and these letters reach out, full of empathy. There were letters from people I didn't know at all, or only by name, welcoming me back to the world and thus simultaneously communicating a very special sense of solidarity. These letters were enormously helpful to me as I was trying to find my footing again. When I began to write this book, I made a note: There will be another abduction. Now, as these pages are on their way to the publisher, there have been at least four abductions and attempted abductions (involving two murders of hostages) which must be classified as replications of mine. Replications which the criminals who abducted me saw coming as a natural consequence of their own crime, and which they built into their calculations with all the pride of trendsetters. Perhaps reading this book will be of use to someone.

My most important reason remained hidden from me for a long time. When I had to allow people to ask why I wanted to publish this book *so soon,* and I asked myself why the act of writing and passing what I'd written around among a few friends and close acquaintances would not be in and of itself sufficient, it finally became clear to me. The answer leads straight to the place that gives the book its title: into the cellar. An abduction, a time beyond all social contact save the antisocial contact with the abductors, is a time of enforced intimacy. A whole code of manners develops, however it comes about. Everybody gets to know one another, not much, but a little. Empathies are present (what can I read in his voice, how serious is it, what can I say to lighten the atmosphere?). All this contained within it an extreme imbalance of power: absolute power over there, absolute helplessness here. That doesn't get left behind in the cellar. For the cellar doesn't get left behind. The cellar will be a permanent part of my life, but as little as possible of the forced intimacy that took place in this cellar should become part of my life. The only weapon against unchosen intimacy is going public.

I know from experience how seductive it can be to be drawn into published accounts written by other people, to read an orderly version of what is still no more than disorder and terror in your own head, for example, in *Spiegel*: "The decisive turn of events is triggered by someone else: Jan Philipp Reemtsma himself, the victim of the abduction. From captivity he sends a letter that brings two new mediators into the game." This, however, as I knew, was purest editorial fantasy. As time went by, I realized how important it is not to integrate such stories into your own story: the truth was something I shared with no one but those who had done this to me and my family. I could be described, in a perverse way, as their accomplice in matters to do with the truth. Along with every trace of intimacy, this special collective complicity is what I must destroy, and the only way to do that is publicly. An inner distance, as I learned, is not sufficient.

My wife and I had wanted to write a book together—but not this one. It was to contain her memories and mine of the thirty-three days; our son would have borne witness to this period in a retrospective conversation, and others who had been involved would have had a hand in it, too. That book, although its main sections did get written, will remain unpublished for the moment.

The conversations about it made clear to me why the question of making things public is different for me from the way it is for my wife or son. For me, it's a matter of destroying an enforced privacy as the prerequisite for being able to view a terrifying episode as a part—however small—of my life and not just as a random self-contained event; for my family, it's a matter of reclaiming the privacy that was destroyed in that period. In a certain sense, during the days of my abduction their entire life was conducted in public. Not for the press—although it too was involved, since it promptly put the house under constant surveillance—but because the house itself was transformed into the center of operations and a permanent conference room. What helped my family to stand fast during this time (whatever that means: when can one be said to have stood fast, when not?) also had this reverse side to it. Friends, relatives, my lawyer, the police—they were always there, without a word of complaint they rearranged their lives in those weeks with the goal of saving my life, supporting my wife with advice and help, and trying through distractions to make what was a time of agonizing uncertainty more bearable for my son. Making a written record of this time was for my wife a step toward reclaiming her privacy, and an attempt to fill out her account with those thoughts and feelings that remain unuttered in the thick of events.

So the two stories, the one about the cellar and the one about what happened outside the cellar, which were supposed to have been combined in the same book, fell away from each other. No final decision has yet been made about publishing the other side of the thirty-three days of my captivity. If the "case" ever gets to court and thus the third side takes visible shape, the perspective may change yet again. The amount of time that will by then have gone by will also make it easier to deal with the problem that while my text is concerned only with things private to me, my wife's text, because of the situation it describes, also touches the private lives of other people.

Nonetheless, I must give what follows some outer structure, which I will limit to a brief chronological presentation in order not to impair the deliberately chosen one-sidedness of my point of view. This text of mine cannot accommodate other perspectives and still present itself as an objective account of what occurred. That would be another book, and one that failed to achieve its own, already stated goal.

On Monday, the twenty-fifth of March 1996, I left our "living-house" at about half past eight to go over to my "work-house"—even these terms wouldn't exist without the abduction; they are the identifying names given to our living arrangements by the police, and which were then taken up nationwide by the press. We do in fact allow ourselves the luxury of living in two houses on the same street, about fifty-five yards from each other. The one house contains my library and private working quarters, the other is where my wife works, and at a certain point my son specified that his room there was indeed to be *his* room. This house also contained an assortment of animals—three cats and two dogs—so that for all intents and purposes it became where we all lived, while the other one became my personal workplace, although the entire family sometimes moves over to it on weekends. This means that it quite frequently happens that when my son switches off his light, I say "Going over," so that I can spend a few hours at my desk. On this particular day we wanted to go to bed early, and I only went over (my wife, as it later turned out, had not even heard me make my usual announcement) to fetch a book.

The abduction had been in the planning for a long time—just how long, by just how many participants and accomplices I don't know. The house with the cellar had been rented in June 1995.

At some point they began to observe my way of life and my habits. As it turned out from a statement given by a witness, at least one of the abductors attended a lecture I gave in Aachen on February 8, 1996, about National Socialism and the Modern. Apparently the abduction was supposed to have taken place at the beginning of March, but that was school vacation time and we were away for two weeks. But at the end of March, evenings were still dark enough.

So I was attacked at the door of the later-named "work-house," knocked down, tied up, led away, and driven off in a car. My wife, first irritated, then made uneasy by the fact that contrary to my usual routine I was spending a long time over at the work-house (as she supposed) without even having mentioned I was going, went out around midnight to see if everything was all right. A statue that stood in front of the house had been knocked over, and on a wall, weighted down with a hand grenade, was an extortion letter:

WE HAVE KIDNAPPED MR. REEMTSMA!

WE DEMAND RANSOM IN THE AMOUNT OF DM
20,000,000

OF THAT, IN SWISS FRANCS 10,000,000

THE REST IN DEUTSCHE MARKS 8,000,000

ONLY USED NOTES—THOUSANDS—NO SERIES
ALTOGETHER 18,000 NOTES
NO MARKING—THEY WILL BE CHECKED
FOR CHEMICAL OR UV-INFRARED TRACES!
INSTRUCTIONS FOR HANDOVER TO FOLLOW
WITH PROOF STILL ALIVE
INVOLVEMENT OF PRESS AND POLICE
MEANS DEATH
IF ALL DEMANDS ARE MET MR
REEMTSMA WILL BE RELEASED
UNHARMED 48 HOURS AFTER RECEIPT OF RANSOM
ARRANGE FOR RANSOM AND WAIT
FOR FURTHER INSTRUCTIONS

My wife, Kathrin Scheerer, first called a mutual friend from Frankfurt and talked over the situation. They both came to the conclusion that the police must be brought in. The friend said he would take care of it. Kathrin then called our friend the lawyer Joachim Kersten, who came immediately with his partner Gerhard Johann Schwenn. Kersten wanted to take charge of organizing the money, Schwenn offered to make himself responsible for contact with the criminals.

Soon the police arrive. Footprints taken. At half past six the next morning Kathrin tells our son Johann what has happened. The friend from Frankfurt arrives at around eight. Shortly afterward, two "family counselors" from the police. At about midday the money is ready. The police bring up the question of marking it. After Kathrin is assured that there is a new method of marking that cannot be detected except by themselves, she agrees. A GPS (global positioning system) is fitted to each of our cars so that if the ransom handover is made, the police can follow the route of the cars. Kathrin signs an authorization for our mail so that any further blackmail letters can be intercepted at the post office. Bugging equipment is installed on the phones in both houses. In the days to come, the house will be home to the two police officials, the two lawyers, the friend from Frankfurt, and relatives—not all of them all the time, but all of them spend a lot of time camping out there, sharing worries, excitement, fear, taking care of Johann and trying to provide distractions for him, giving advice on what to do and how to proceed.

Wednesday, March 27. A letter from the abductors, containing the desired Polaroid.

IF YOU ARE READY TO PAY RANSOM
OF DM 20,000,000 OF WHICH
10,000,000 IN SWISS FRANCS
ONLY IN DENOMINATIONS
OF THOUSAND SEE LETTER ON
FRONT DOOR TO PAY PLACE ANNOUNCEMENT
IN *HAMBURG MORNING POST* IN HAMBURG
GREETINGS COLUMN WITH TEXT ALL
GOOD WISHES ANN KATHRIN GET IN
TOUCH AND GIVE FAX NUMBER

With the help of the police, the text of an announcement is worked out and delivered to the *Hamburg Morning Post,* which from now on will delay the closing of the announcements column, at the request of the police, for contact ads of this kind. The text of the announcement (in order to encourage a further sign of life): "All good wishes Ann Kathrin/Get in touch/Are you really fine?/Fax 866 36 59."

Thursday, March 28. The announcement appears in slightly altered form. "All good wishes Ann Kathrin/ Get in touch with me personally/Fax 866 36 59." It's not clear why the police changed the text or were not able to transmit it correctly. Resolution: work together with the police on everything from now on. A second announcement, for the next day, is worded: "All good wishes Ann Kathrin/Get in touch/Fax 866 36 59/ Don't worry." A second letter from the blackmailers arrives:

YOU HAVE BROUGHT IN THE POLICE

THIS WAS AN ERROR

IF YOU WANT TO SEE YOUR HUSBAND ALIVE

AGAIN TAKE CARE THAT NO

SEARCH TAKES PLACE BEFORE HIS

RELEASE

IF THE CURRENT SEARCH FOR WHEREABOUTS

CONTINUES WE WILL DIG IN AND

YOUR HUSBAND WILL HAVE TO ENDURE

FOR WEEKS IN HIS SITUATION

IF THE POLICE ARE PRESENT IN

ANY WAY AT TRANSFER OF MONEY

WE WILL SET A HARDER PACE

IT WILL BE HARDEST

FOR YOUR HUSBAND

This message came with two handwritten letters from the cellar. (I will introduce and discuss the texts of my letters at a later point. They have very little bearing on what was happening outside the cellar.) Discussion as to who should make the money drop. For obvious reasons, our son is adamant that his mother not be the one to hand over the money in any circumstances. She promises him that if she has to go, she will not do so alone.

Friday, March 29. The next letter from the blackmailers:

WE HAVE SEEN THE ANNOUNCEMENT
WE ASSUME FROM THIS THAT YOU HAVE
THE MONEY READY AS PER OUR DEMAND
AND ARE READY TO PAY THERE IS
NO REASON TO MAKE PERSONAL CONTACT
WE HAVE GIVEN YOU SUFFICIENT PROOF
THAT YOUR HUSBAND IS WELL IF
YOU FOLLOW OUR INSTRUCTIONS EXACTLY
NOTHING WILL HAPPEN TO ANYONE
WE WANT THE MONEY DELIVERED BY
ANN KATHRIN SCHEERER IN PERSON AND
ALONE USE YOUR HUSBAND'S VOLVO
GET AN ORANGE FLASHING LIGHT
TO INSTALL ON THE ROOF THAT
YOU CAN CONTROL FROM THE
CIGARETTE LIGHTER
PLACE THE MONEY ON THE PASSENGER
SEAT

HIDE THE MONEY IN A NYLON

BAG WITH A SHOULDER STRAP

THE MONEY WILL NOT BE IN BUNDLES

OR HAVE ANY OF THE PREVIOUSLY

LISTED MARKERS OR BE EQUIPPED

WITH A TRANSMITTER!!!

THE POLICE WILL NOT ACCOMPANY

YOU IN PLAIN CLOTHES OR ANY

OTHER WAY OR OBSERVE YOU

IF A HELICOPTER OR AN UNMARKED

CAR OR ANY KIND OF POLICE VEHICLE

FOLLOWS YOU WE WILL IMMEDIATELY

BREAK CONTACT

THE CONSEQUENCES OF RADIO BEACON

HELICOPTER OR POLICE MOVEMENTS

WILL FALL ON YOUR HUSBAND

THE SAME GOES FOR THE POLICE: IF WE

ARE DISTURBED DURING OR AFTER THE

MONEY DROP WE WILL OPEN FIRE WITHOUT

WARNING

WE WILL SEND YOU A FAX AT 886 36 59

SHORTLY BEFORE THE DROP

LEAVE IN YOUR CAR IMMEDIATELY

AND STICK TO THE DIRECTIONS

YOU WILL BE IN NO DANGER IF YOU

DO AS WE ASK

STARTING MONDAY AT 7 P.M. BE READY

EACH NIGHT FROM 7 P.M. TO 6 A.M.

IF EVERYTHING GOES SMOOTHLY YOUR

HUSBAND WILL BE FREE 48 HOURS LATER

Another announcement is written in order to bring Gerhard Johann Schwenn into play as the money carrier. The police are in favor of using a member of the secret service, but Schwenn remains the choice. The money comes to the house. It is marked. Kathrin includes a letter with it, containing a plea to shorten the forty-eight-hour interval. The police believe the house to be under observation by the press. The police are keeping them informed of the status of things on a daily basis, with the understanding that they will exercise restraint and not publish anything. This procedure works.

Saturday, March 30. The announcement appears: "All good wishes Ann Kathrin/I need a signal/I am exhausted, I cannot manage it/Gerhard is doing everything for me/He can also manage it earlier/Please get in touch/Fax 866 36 59." Another letter arrives from the abductors:

DEAR MR POLICE PSYCHOLOGIST
WE HAVE READ YOUR ANNOUNCEMENT
YOU WILL FIND OUT SOON ENOUGH
HOW MANY PERPETRATORS THERE ARE
EVERYTHING WILL REMAIN AS WE
HAVE DEMANDED
MS SCHEERER WILL DELIVER THE
MONEY WE WILL CONTACT YOU
BY FAX 866 36 59 OR BY PHONE
866 31 44 OR 866 31 58
BE READY
IF THE TRANSFER GOES WRONG

BECAUSE OF POLICE TACTICS OR IF
AN ASSAULT IS ATTEMPTED WE
WILL CUT OFF ONE OF MR REEMTSMA'S
FINGERS HE ALREADY HAS A BROKEN
NOSE OTHERWISE EVERYTHING REMAINS
AS PREVIOUSLY COMMUNICATED

In case something should happen to her during the money drop, Kathrin writes a farewell letter to our son. In the evening, a conference with Michael Daleki and Dieter Langendörfer, the leader of the "S(pecial) T(ask Force) Reemtsma." Reassurances that the police will adhere strictly to the so-called fulfillment concept (the absolute priority is the life of the hostage; fulfillment of the extortionists' demands; no search until either release or death).

Sunday, March 31. After the last letter from the kidnappers, the police ask for an extension of their authorization so that they can intercept packages as well as mail. Kathrin is questioned about the possible background of the crime.

Slowly the news percolates its way via the usual have-you-heard and press requests for information to the Hamburg Institute for Social Research,* where until now the fiction has been sustained of a sudden trip abroad. Colleagues are gradually informed one by one. But nothing—which is unusual for a place with forty people working full-time—leaks out to the public.

*Author heads this institute.

Monday, April 1. Announcement: "All good wishes Ann Kathrin/Gerhard is ready to start, if I know that all's well with you/Get in touch/Fax 866 36 59."

Letter from kidnappers:

IF GERHARD REFERS TO LAWYER JOHANN

SCHWENN HE CAN ACCOMPANY MS SCHEERER

TO THE DROP

OTHERWISE EVERYTHING REMAINS AS STIPULATED

BE READY AT THE RELEVANT TIMES AND

FOLLOW OUR DEMANDS EXACTLY

IF DONE YOUR HUSBAND WILL BE BACK

AT HOME FOR EASTER

It is accompanied by another two handwritten pages from the cellar. Kathrin completes a test drive with the GPS. Telephone call from *Bild Zeitung*. Request to publish an appeal to the kidnappers. Meanwhile, members of the press are populating the street in front of our house, with and without cameras.

Tuesday, April 2. In the morning, publication of announcement: "All good wishes Ann Kathrin/Tell me, why haven't you sent me a picture?/Everything fine with me/Get in touch/Fax: you have my number already." During the day, another handwritten letter arrives from the cellar. The next day's announcement is drafted: "All good wishes Ann Kathrin/We will both do what you want/Don't keep us waiting so long without anything to see or read. How are things going?/Get in touch/Fax: you have the number." 2:45 a.m.; phone call from the kidnappers, taken by Schwenn. The kidnappers use a voice-distortion device, are almost incomprehensible. It takes frequent replaying of the recording to make out the message: Drive to highway on-ramp Bahrenfeld, pick up a message at crossroads there. No crossroads visible on road map. Kathrin and Johann Schwenn are taken there; the GPS-equipped car is waiting there under police surveillance, but the car that brings them is late and has to run red lights because there is so little time. The crossroads turns out to be the beginning of a path, only reachable on foot. There, behind an electric junction box, the next notice in a clear plastic container attached with duct tape.

SWITCH ON FLASHING LIGHT AND LEAVE
ON
GO THROUGH ELBE TUNNEL IN DIRECTION
OF HANNOVER
DO NOT DRIVE FASTER THAN 50 MPH
AND ONLY IN SLOW LANE
DO NOT OVERTAKE
WHEN YOU SEE ANOTHER BLINKING ORANGE
LIGHT STOP THE CAR
TAKE THE MONEY AND HOOK THE
BAG TO THE ORANGE ROPE NEXT TO
THE BLINKER
WHEN FINISHED DRIVE ON IMMEDIATELY
IF YOU DO NOT SEE BLINKING LIGHT
STOP AT SIGN FOR MASCHEN 2 1/2
MILES ON AND PICK UP SECOND MESSAGE

Journey takes place as per instructions. No blinking light to be seen, before sign for "Maschen." No further instructions on sign or on guardrail. Return after conversation with the police.

Wednesday, April 3. Yesterday's announcement is printed; the next day's is composed: "All good wishes Ann Kathrin/What is going on?/Get in touch/You have the numbers."

Thursday, April 4. No letter from the abductors but another two letters from the cellar—one to Kathrin, one to Schwenn—in Kathrin's notes, the "panic letters." 11 p.m. call from the blackmailers, this time much easier to understand. Problems on their side, no one able to come. There will be a call the next night between 9 and 11 p.m.; there's also a question set for Schwenn to answer by way of identifying himself.

Easter Friday, April 5. No call.

Easter Saturday, April 6. Announcement: "All good wishes Ann Kathrin/Why haven't you come?/Nothing will happen to you/The waiting is unbearable/Get in touch. You have the numbers." The police assume I am probably dead, and ask a friend of the family (if this turns out to be true) to tell my wife. In order to find out if I am still alive, an announcement is composed for the next day's paper which contains a question out of our private family language. "All good wishes Ann Kathrin/Tell me: what's the name of Benni's legs again? Call me today without fail/Everything has been ready for days/You have my numbers." 3 a.m. phone call. Because of the extreme voice distortion, it takes Schwenn two repetitions of the code question before he can answer (the question is about an impediment suffered by a teacher known to us both from our school days). Nothing else. Phone call to follow "in the next few days."

Easter Sunday, April 7. Nothing.

Easter Monday, April 8. Kathrin decides that the next time the kidnappers call, she will speak to them herself. No call.

Tuesday, April 9. The announcement composed on the sixth is printed. Another question is formulated to prove I'm alive: "All good wishes Ann Kathrin/I have forgotten the nicknames of our two houses/What are they?/Get in touch today/I would like to make the trip at long last/You have the numbers."

Wednesday, April 10. Letter from the abductors:

AS LONG AS WE HAVE REASON TO BELIEVE
YOU ARE WORKING WITH THE POLICE MR
SCHWENN IT WILL BE A LONG TIME
BEFORE THIS THING IS OVER
WE HAVE AMPLE TIME
YOU SHOULD THINK ABOUT WHOSE
INTERESTS YOU ARE PURSUING
BECAUSE WE HAD TO ABORT THE
SECOND ATTEMPT AT THE DROP AS
WELL BECAUSE OF POLICE PRESENCE
THERE WILL BE NO FURTHER ATTEMPT
IN HAMBURG AREA
ALL THIS IS UNNECESSARILY PROLONGING THE
SUFFERING OF YOUR CLIENT
WE HAVE NO INTEREST IN FURTHER PHONE

CONVERSATIONS WITH THE POLICE PSYCHOLOGIST
OBTAIN A CELLULAR TELEPHONE FROM
SOMEONE YOU KNOW AND GIVE US THE
NUMBER WHEN NEXT CONTACTED ON
WEDNESDAY
WE WILL THEN DIRECT YOU TO A NEUTRAL
TELEPHONE (AFTER 9 P.M.)
IN ADDITION HIRE A ONE-ENGINE PLANE (CESSNA)
SUITABLE FOR AERIAL MONEY DROP
PACK THE MONEY ACCORDINGLY
THE PLANE SHOULD BE READY ON
THURSDAY AND FRIDAY AFTER 6 P.M. FOR
FLIGHT AT 1,000 TO 18,800 FEET
WE WILL TELL YOU THE FLIGHT COORDINATES
BEFOREHAND E.G. BY CELLULAR PHONE DURING THE
    FLIGHT
THIS WILL BE THE LAST ATTEMPT FOR
A LONG TIME
IF THIS ATTEMPT GOES WRONG THE
RANSOM DEMAND GOES UP BY TEN
MILLION MARKS
IF WE SHOULD HAVE TO CONCLUDE THAT
IT IS TOO RISKY TO PICK UP THE
MONEY WE WILL KILL MR REEMTSMA
THINK VERY CAREFULLY ABOUT WHAT
YOU DECIDE TO DO
THE PLANE MUST HAVE A RANGE OF
500–750 MILES AND BE ABLE TO MAINTAIN LAND
    SPEED OF
125 MPH

This is accompanied by two more letters from the cellar. In one of them is a reference to the kidnappers' opinion that it was not Schwenn on the phone last time but a police official who was passing on the question to Schwenn—hence the delay in Schwenn's reply. A suitable plane is found and refitted for this special use. A pilot prepares for the trip. Schwenn is given instruction on how to throw out the money. Phone call shortly before 11 p.m. Kathrin speaks, alludes to the voice-distortion device; says there was no one from the police on the line; says the instructions will be followed. Reply: In an hour's time, at midnight, Mr. Schwenn should be in the Atlantic Hotel, hand in his card at reception, and wait. Trip to hotel. Phone call there; Schwenn should go to Hotel Ibis across the street and wait for the next phone call. Another test question is posed. This time without problem. Then a whole series of questions is reviewed in what might almost be described as a peaceful discussion: why didn't the drops work (again: the car is said to have arrived too late); could one not negotiate at some time other than midnight; how was the hostage (fine); might they perhaps care to hurry up a little so that all this could be brought to an end; did the interval after the money changed hands really have to be forty-eight hours (this was the "upper limit"); how would things now proceed? "In the next few days."

Thursday, April 11. In the meantime, news of the abduction had become the topic of the day in more places than Hamburg. There are phone calls, letters, offers of help from friends and acquaintances. There are messages from members of families who have had experience of kidnappings, full of advice and assistance. The police arrange for a changing series of announcements to run until April 27, with texts in various combinations such as: "I am waiting," "Do it soon," "Get in touch," "What is happening?" etc., and also containing further questions to ascertain if I am alive. They seem to have no noticeable effect on communication with the perpetrators.

Friday, April 12. Nothing.

Saturday, April 13. Morning phone call from the kidnappers. Schwenn is instructed to drive to Luxembourg—a route is laid down. He is to take a room in a particular hotel and wait for further instructions. Schwenn observes that he is a slow driver and will need time. Okay. When can he leave? In one—gesticulations from the policewoman beside him—no, two hours. In the company of a female colleague whom he will set down before the frontier is reached. This too is accepted. The "colleague," as indicated above a policewoman, is late. She has forgotten her passport, as it later turns out. The official version given to my wife and Mr. Schwenn is that the GPS, which has meantime been fitted to Schwenn's car, suddenly fell out. Night: the abductors make contact in the Hotel Luxembourg, ask a further question for purposes of identification which Schwenn, because the voice-distortion device is in use again, misunderstands and answers wrong. Nonetheless, he is instructed to drive to a nearby gas station and receive a further message. It runs:

> DRIVE AT APPROX 50 MPH ON THE
> HIGHWAY TO TRIER
> STOP AT THE FIRST REST STOP AFTER
> THE GERMAN BORDER.
> IT IS CALLED MARKUSBERG (APPROX 3 MILES)
> SECOND MESSAGE IS THERE
> WHEN YOU COME INTO THE REST STOP
> BEAR SHARP RIGHT
> THERE IS A LARGE IRON GATE (RIGHT
> AT THE ENTRANCE TO THE PARKING LOT)
> THE MESSAGE IS ON THE RIGHT HAND GATE POST

There:

> THROW THE MONEY OVER THE FENCE TO
> THE RIGHT OF THE GATE
> DRIVE ON IMMEDIATELY
> DRIVE TO THE EXIT FOR KOBLENZ/
> SAARBRÜCKEN/TRIER
> TURN ROUND THERE AND DRIVE BACK
> TO THE HOTEL
> IF WE HAVE ANY PROBLEMS PICKING UP
> THE MONEY WE WILL CALL YOU THERE
> IF WE DO NOT CALL
> EVERYTHING IS OKAY
> WITHIN 48 HOURS MAXIMUM MR R
> WILL BE WITH YOU

Message to Hamburg: everything has gone according to plan.

Saturday, April 14. The money has not been picked up. Police disguised as tourists have checked this out after several hours. The reason for the failure of the handover remains unclear. Tension and anger building between Mr. Schwenn and the police. Kathrin announces she will go alone next time. If a companion is necessary, then with the friend from Frankfurt, who says he is ready to go. Kathrin orders the police to remove all apparatus from the cars. Next time there is to be no police activity whatsoever.

Monday, April 15. A new announcement for the next day's paper: "All good wishes Ann Kathrin/I am doing everything you want/What is wrong? We both want the same thing—as quickly as possible/Get in touch." That evening Michael Herrmann, a close acquaintance with whom I had been active in city politics, arrives at the door. Herrmann tells Kathrin in the absence of the police that the kidnappers have phoned Pastor Christian Arndt, who belonged to this same group, and someone whom he doesn't know named Professor Clausen, to ask if they would be ready to act as carriers for the money. This is to be the last attempt; the names are ones I proposed.

Thursday, April 16. A gathering of the full staff at the Hamburg Institute for Social Research so that Joachim Kersten can update all my colleagues on where things stand. Herrmann—under the pretext of paying a visit to encourage everyone—reports that the letters from the cellar affirmed that the proposal really

did originate with the kidnappers, that Arndt and
Clausen have been authorized to act as carriers by
me, and slips Kathrin a copy of the abductors' letter
to Arndt and also an accompanying letter to her and
Johann. The abductors write:

DEAR PASTOR ARNDT

DEAR DR CLAUSEN

MANY THANKS FOR YOUR WILLINGNESS

TO ACT AS GO-BETWEENS

I ASSURE YOU THAT THERE WILL

BE NO DANGER FOR YOU

AS YOU ALREADY KNOW WE HAVE

ABDUCTED MR REEMTSMA AND AFTER

THREE FAILED ATTEMPTS (BECAUSE

OF POLICE TACTICS) TO ARRANGE

THE EXCHANGE OF MONEY WE

NOW DEMAND 30 MILLION DEUTSCHE MARKS

RANSOM* HALF

IN SWISS FRANCS AND HALF IN

DM, ONLY UNMARKED BILLS IN

DENOMINATIONS OF ONE THOUSAND

MR REEMTSMA IS IN GOOD PHYSICAL

HEALTH

I GIVE YOU MY WORD THAT MR

REEMTSMA WILL BE RELEASED

UNINJURED 48 HOURS AFTER WE

HAVE RECEIVED THE RANSOM

PAYMENT

*$20 million at 1996 rate of exchange.

THE POLICE WILL HAVE TOLD YOU
THAT WE WILL KILL MR REEMTSMA
ANYWAY
THIS IS NOT TRUE!
NO VICTIM HAS EVER BEEN KILLED
AFTER PAYMENT OF A HIGH RANSOM
IT WILL NOT HAPPEN THIS TIME EITHER
WE VIEW THIS AS A BUSINESS TRANSACTION
AND WILL HONOR ALL FULFILLED AGREEMENTS
BUT I ALSO GIVE YOU MY WORD
THAT WE WILL KILL MR REEMTSMA
IF CURRENT TACTICS CONTINUE
OUR PATIENCE ALSO HAS ITS LIMITS
I THEREFORE ASK YOU IN THE INTERESTS
OF US ALL TO BRING THIS MATTER
TO A SPEEDY CONCLUSION
AGAIN I GUARANTEE YOU THAT WE
WILL FOLLOW ALL AGREED PROCEDURES
TO THE LETTER AND DO NOT PLAY
DOUBLE GAMES THE WAY SCHWENN
THE LAWYER DOES

Why the kidnappers listed three attempted ex-changes instead of the actual two is unclear.

It is agreed not to notify the police. But because Herrmann's appearance is bound to arouse suspicion, the impression should be created that he has been named as a new money carrier by the kidnappers in order to focus any possible police surveillance, which could be picked up by the kidnappers, on him.

Wednesday, April 17. Michael Herrmann surreptitiously brings a cellular phone so that calls can be made without police supervision. Arndt and Clausen are similarly equipped. Another ten million Deutsche marks has to be organized, and in order for Arndt and Clausen to be able to get at the money without the knowledge of the police, the entire amount has to be mobilized all over again. Our New York trustee and our lawyer there take charge of these financial arrangements and announce they will be on their way in a few hours.

Various further announcements are arranged and the press is kept up to date—with the same information the police have. Meanwhile, press helicopters periodically fly over the house. An illustrated magazine demands access to the archives of my old school, which is refused by the director.

Thursday, April 18. Message from Michael Herrmann: the letter to Clausen has also arrived in the meantime (it took longer because it was addressed to the University of Kiel). The American trustees arrive. They have made contact with the private security service ESPO, the German branch of an American firm. Michael Herrmann announces that a new letter from the abductors has reached Arndt and Clausen:

DEAR DR CLAUSEN

DEAR PASTOR ARNDT

I ASSUME YOU HAVE RECEIVED OUR LETTERS

AND PERHAPS HAVE ALREADY MET EACH

OTHER YOU WILL CERTAINLY ALSO HAVE

DISCUSSED THE MATTER WITH MS

SCHEERER HER LAWYER AND THE

POLICE

THE AFFAIR CAN ONLY BE WITHOUT

BLOODSHED IF THE RANSOM IS PAID

WITHOUT THE INVOLVEMENT OF THE POLICE

YOU MUST REGARD THE WHOLE THING

AS A BUSINESS MATTER

WHOEVER PAYS GOES FREE WHOEVER

DOES NOT PAY DIES

OUR PATIENCE WILL SOON RUN OUT BECAUSE

THE WHOLE THING IS ALREADY ENTERING ITS

FOURTH WEEK IF CURRENT POLICE

TACTICS CONTINUE THIS WILL MEAN

THE CERTAIN DEATH OF MR REEMTSMA

WE WILL ADDRESS ALL WRITTEN

COMMUNICATIONS TO MR CLAUSEN'S

ADDRESS

PASTOR ARNDT PLEASE OBTAIN A

CELLULAR PHONE FROM SOMEONE YOU

KNOW WHICH WILL NOT BE CONNECTED

TO THE POLICE

I WILL CALL YOU AT HOME ON FRIDAY

AT 8 P.M. AND DIRECT YOU TO A HOTEL

I WILL PLACE A CALL TO RECEPTION

THEN YOU CAN GIVE ME THE NUMBER

WE HOPE THE WHOLE THING CAN SOON

BE CONCLUDED WITH YOUR HELP

WITHOUT BLOODSHED

Kathrin decides that the police must leave the house and be seen to do so, in case of surveillance. The police are told that Herrmann is the new money carrier. The next drop will be made without informing them. Whereupon the officials offer to leave the house. Kathrin agrees.

Friday, April 19. Conversation with Michael Daleki about the decision to proceed from now on without any police involvement. The money is delivered to Clausen in anticipation of a call from the kidnappers. The kidnappers call Arndt. He is to go to a particular telephone booth, where there will be another phone call with questions to establish identity. The kidnappers swear on the telephone that nobody has played straight with them so far. Nothing more.

Saturday, April 20. Meeting with representatives from ESPO. Urgent advice to break off the game of conspiracy. "The only way to do without the police is to work with the police." ESPO takes over dealings with the police. The prepared money is moved from the house to the bank.

Sunday, April 21. Evening meeting between Kathrin, the trustees, and Daleki. Discussion of what comes next. Kathrin decides against any further marking of the money—most of all to protect the new messengers from possible revenge later on. The police will be informed that every bank note has been photocopied. The police will receive the serial numbers when I am free. The police tell ESPO that they give my chances of surviving the abduction as 60/40 against.

Monday, April 22. The banker Max Warburg arranges an appointment for Kathrin with the mayor, Henning Voscherau.

Tuesday, April 23. Meeting with Voscherau. Explanation of the now agreed-upon strategy in the hope that Voscherau will bind the police to support this course of action.

Wednesday, April 24. 11:10 p.m. call from kidnappers. Arndt and Clausen ask a proof-of-life question—where one of our cats came from. The answer, "Trittau," becomes a code word between the kidnappers and the couriers. Arndt and Clausen are instructed to take Highway AI toward Bremen/Osnabrück/Münster and to wait for further telephone directions. They receive a call on the cellular phone telling them to collect the next message from a right-of-way sign by the merging lane at the Münsterland rest stop.

CODE WORD TRITTAU

CONTINUE ON HIGHWAY 1

TO THE KAMEN INTERCHANGE

TAKE THE A2 IN DIRECTION
    RECKUNGHAUSEN/OBERHAUSEN

FOLLOW A2 TO DUISBURG/KAISERSBERG INTERCHANGE

THEN SWITCH TO A40 IN DIRECTION OF

DUISBURG/VENLO

FOLLOW A40 TO INTERCHANGE MOERS/KAPELLEN

TAKE THE A57 IN DIRECTION NEUSS/COLOGNE

FOLLOW A57 UNTIL WE CALL YOU OR

UNTIL YOU REACH GEISMÜHLE REST AREA

(JUST PAST KREFELD)
WAIT THERE UNTIL YOU RECEIVE NEW
INSTRUCTIONS

There's a phone call telling them where the next message is to be found—on another traffic sign. It runs:

CODE WORD TRITTAU
I ASSURE YOU AGAIN THAT
YOU WILL BE IN NO DANGER IF YOU
FOLLOW OUR INSTRUCTIONS EXACTLY
PROCEED IMMEDIATELY ALONG A57 TO
NEXT INTERCHANGE
IT IS CALLED STRÜMP
TAKE THE A44 IN DIRECTION OF
WILLICH/MÖNCHENGLADBACH
TAKE THE FIRST EXIT TO 26 MEERBUSCH/OSTERRATH
WHEN YOU GET TO THE FOOT OF
THE EXIT RAMP TURN RIGHT
AFTER APPROX 50–75 YARDS THERE
IS AN ASPHALTED SIDE ROAD TO THE
LEFT TAKE THIS ROAD
FOLLOW IT FOR APPROX 75 YARDS
UNTIL YOU COME TO A FORK
STOP THERE AND SWITCH OFF HEADLIGHTS
LEAVE KEY IN IGNITION
LEAVE MONEY IN CAR AND GET OUT
WALK BACK TO MAIN ROAD AND
TURN LEFT IN DIRECTION KREFELD/STEINRATH
DO NOT STOP OR TURN ROUND

WALK UNTIL YOU REACH POST OFFICE
CALL FOR A TAXI AND WAIT UNTIL
WE CALL YOU
WE WILL INFORM YOU WHETHER WE
WERE ABLE TO PICK UP MONEY AND
WHERE YOU WILL FIND YOUR CAR
PICK UP YOUR CAR AND DRIVE HOME
IF EVERYTHING HAS GONE WELL MR R
WILL BE WITH YOU ON FRIDAY NIGHT

Arndt and Clausen receive word by telephone that everything has gone according to plan for the kidnappers except that unfortunately they have totaled the car in the dark. The extortionists make a point of apologizing for this disaster.

Thursday, April 25. In the morning, the American trustees inform my wife that the money has successfully changed hands. In the early hours of Saturday morning I then called home.

So—thus far, the driest account of what took place outside the cellar. While all this was playing itself out, my place was not in that world—I was behind the "stay out" sign. And if I now begin to describe what it was like "being outside" behind the cellar door, I also worry about the place in the world that this experience occupies. I am afraid that this too must remain "outside."

Not only does it have nothing to do with the drama

just described, it also has nothing to do with any other experience (except for those undergone by others who have experienced it, or something like it). There is no way to get at it. It teaches nothing. That you do not attack a person, drag him away, smash his head against the wall, chain him up, hold him in isolation and in fear of his life for weeks on end, is already a well-known fact. I did not come home with any revelations about it.

What follows is an attempt to describe this "outsideness," an experiment in giving form to this occurrence (I don't want to call it "experience," because experiences are related to the continuity of life, and this is about portraying what it is like to undergo extreme *dis*continuity and the feelings that go with it) as far as may be possible—and that is not very far at all. Because I know from letters sent by people who have been through something similar that it's like forming your own family: you feel very close, and yet you also see from the letters that there's a limit on what they can articulate; nonetheless, you know and they know what is *not* being talked about. Thus I know that I will have a few readers who will understand immediately the paradoxes inherent in attempting to write such an account. As for all the others, I can only ask their understanding that I have made no attempt to fire the reader's imagination with vivid metaphors and a particularly lively narrative style; I do not regard the writing of this account as being primarily a literary endeavor. It largely abstains from literary devices, most particularly it abjures all fictional license. What you will read in the following pages happened that way—or at least is remembered that way.

The goal of this book—to destroy an intimacy that was forced upon me—obliges me not only to be as honest as I possibly can, but also puts me in a situation that I would otherwise consider to smack of something approaching exhibitionism. It cannot be helped. But I did think it would be helpful in the following pages to write of myself in the third person. It was easier to put painful things into words this way: moreover, this stylized figure is congruent with the fact that there is no continuity between the "I" of my desk and the "I" of the cellar whom I shall have to describe.

I would like to begin with the cellar where he was chained for thirty-three days. Or perhaps with the car journey that took me there for the second time. A warm day in early summer; I was in an unmarked police car. The police had told me they were 90 percent certain that they had found the right cellar, but required my presence to make an absolutely positive identification. The cellar was not in the region of Soltau where they had been searching for the last few days, but near Bremen. This did not fit with a memory that I had of his return journey in the trunk of the car, but did fit with another memory, which in turn did not tally with the stretch of highway between Soltau and Hamburg. The trip lasted longer than he remembered the first journey being. I asked: If they were going to show me a cellar and ask me to identify it, then presumably they had found the holes for the planking that boarded up the windows and for the chain that was dowelled into the wall, and to which he had been shackled for thirty-three days; if not, there was no reason for the journey. Yes, they had found them, although the cellar had only one window—the other one had just been faked by more planking. And there were other things that didn't entirely fit with my report.

I wondered what my son would say now. In the last few days, he was the one who had been something of a professional pessimist. "They'll never find them—too much evidence was destroyed." He would probably say it was not the right cellar but another one that had just been fixed up that way to lay a false trail. (And in fact my son that evening said exactly that.) In the unlikely event that a second prepared cellar really did exist, could I recognize the real one? I remembered that there had been a gouge in the plaster next to the mattress, which he had always looked at and tried to describe before going to sleep. A kind of blunted half-moon that he could have stuck two fingertips into. "There's a mark—if I see it, I'll know it's the cellar," I said to my companion, and described the place. I was thinking of an eventual trial and the insinuation of a lawyer for the defense that I had noticed the place in the plaster only after I got there. "If the cellar has been replastered, I can't say if I'll be able to recognize it again for sure."

We arrived. On the last stretch of the road I closed my eyes. Is this how the approach had been? Something like it. But exactly? Car comes to a stop. Get out. Path to the house. Is that how it had felt? Perhaps. The house—a vacation house. Thatched roof. Big garden, sufficiently out-of-the-way. In the cellar of this house? . . . For whatever reason, he had imagined something like an unfinished new building. One step up; correct. Front room. "Now you turn right to go down to the cellar." Wrong, it was the kitchen. The cellar was to the left. Could he have confused left and right? As he had been led out, he had been made to turn around several times—had that happened when he was led in as well, and I had forgotten? How easy is it to disorient a frightened, bound, blindfolded man, who is nonetheless still somewhat in possession of his senses? Fairly easy, apparently.

The entrance to the cellar, the steps. Yes, those were the steps. Made of wood, turning slightly to the right. I knew the steps, what it felt like to go down them, the noises. "Now you go left into the room." I turned left, there was a cellar room. I felt someone was making a fool of me: the radiator on the wrong side, the proportions of the room all wrong, the room too small. It was like being in a bad dream. "Please look around again, look at the whole cellar." Why? To the right, a furnace room. Round a corner, to the left, another room, take a look around. Door fits, heating unit fits, proportions fit. There are the wall sockets. It looks smaller. Light-bulb in the middle of the ceiling, ceiling height fits, too. One window. There are traces of badly filled holes in the wall where the windows were covered over. Where is the place where the chain was fixed in? The place in the plaster, is it there? Yes. There it is. With pointed finger: "That's the spot I told you about. This is the cellar." Yes, that's where the chain was. I lay down. Yes, the spot in the plaster, the blunted half-moon shape was where it had been. I touched it with my index finger and middle finger. Yes, this was the room where he had spent thirty-three days in fear of his life and worse. Then I stood up, the faces of the police officials around me revealed a mixture of joy and sympathy and, it seemed to me, respect. I was confused for a moment, couldn't think why. Later I understood that it was when they saw this room that some of them had for the first time revised their idea of the "deluxe kidnapping"—an expression that one of the criminals had used, and that I had reported myself and the press had greedily adopted—and could imagine that this return to the cellar was a profoundly ambiguous experience for me. Apparently this must have showed. Perhaps I had served as a kind of Nancy Drew experience for them, which is not so common in the daily routine of criminologists.

They took a statement, and while I was answering their questions, I walked back and forth in the cellar. The movements gave me back my feeling for the room. Yes, that's how long the chain was: if he leaned here with his left hand, stood on his left leg and reached his right hand as far as possible along the chain, he could touch the thermostat on the radiator. There must be finger marks on the wall, he had been given newspapers and gotten ink on his fingers. No, the walls were whitewashed. But sloppily. Someone had just brushed over them. Then there must—yes, that was where he had leaned against the wall for a sort of angled support: there too the all-too-visible traces had been whited over. Yes, the size of the room was right: if the space had been larger, the toilet would not have been next to the door, and he would not have reached the socket on the opposite wall from the chain.

And this blunted half-moon shape. He had looked at it again and again, and at a certain point had wondered what it was about this spot in the plaster that so fascinated him. It had reminded him of a passage in one of Enid Blyton's Famous Five books, in which a secret door is discovered: suddenly hands grope and find a notch in the paneling, and the wall opens up. His fingers had remembered this spot, and as they touched the plaster had expressed the desire to escape by secret magic. But then there would still be the chain, and so not even that would help me, he had thought at the time. But he had remembered a lot of children's books with secret doors, most of all Josephine Siebe's *Little Caspar in the Castle,* in which there's a "little secret door" that can be opened with a clothes hanger that twists, so that you can sneak in and out; later little Caspar, too, gets locked in a cellar, and he finds a secret door there also, but it doesn't lead outside, it goes to the wine cellar, and little Caspar drinks up all the Count's favorite wine.

If I survive this, he had sometimes thought to himself in the cellar, then I will write something about it and begin with a quotation from *Little Caspar in the Castle.* And then I will write something about the fantasies of prisoners. And about this spot in the plaster. But how will I describe it? "Half-moon" isn't right, it's too flattened for that, like a vanilla horn at Christmas (but how well known is this pastry and the particular shape I mean? Besides, vanilla horns are more curved). Don't those things that get nailed under the tips of your shoes to reinforce them and then make that awful noise on wooden floors—don't they look like that?

I remembered these thoughts as I was forced to remember the place, and the mark was visible to the so-called inner eye. As I looked around a little after giving the statement, I noticed all the things he could have noticed, if they had crossed his mind. But the flattened half-moon had been enough. I looked around once more and then left: what an utterly ordinary place! How was this standard cellar with two double electric outlets, a bulb in the ceiling, and a radiator with a thermostat next to the door connected in any way with the thirty-three days? This discrepancy suddenly shook me physically to the core, and I turned back once more. Some sign on the walls aside from the marks and the flattened half-moon that could be recognized again, something like a piece of demonic handwriting, anything except the banality of this cellar, and over there is the central heating, and next to it is where you wash your hands. But nothing. Eventually I left. Outside, the early summer weather. When they had tied him up and brought him here, it was March 25 and the little pond in front of his house was still frozen.

He had been supposed to fly to the United States, to St. Louis, to a conference on postwar German literature. He was supposed to have given a lecture there, and was still working on it. The last text he had finished work on a few days before his abduction was an editorial for an issue of our journal of the Hamburg

Institute for Social Research, on the theme of "traumatization." Part of the text said:

"After severe mechanical accidents, such as train collisions, when there are life-threatening injuries, a condition has long been noted that is still known as traumatic neurosis. The terrible war that has just ended* produced a large number of such illnesses." When the severely traumatized were asleep, the events that released the trauma surfaced in their dreams and reproduced their terror. A finding that seemed incompatible with the pleasure principle as the dominating factor in dreams. This compulsive connection with the traumatic event is something other than what we normally call "memory." Even in normal therapy there is always the return to the necessity, as Freud says, "to repeat the repressed as contemporary experience, instead of recalling it, as the doctor would prefer, as a part of the past."

Here we may glimpse an indication of the traumatic root of this neurosis, but it also shows the difference between this and extreme traumatization. If the reliving of the repressed is the so-called normal neurotic part of the healing process, the deeply traumatized person remains psychologically shackled to the traumatizing event; it haunts him in nightmares, suddenly overwhelms him in so-called flashbacks. This terroristic presence of the past is accompanied by its psychic extraterritoriality, by an inability to work through the

*World War I.

event, to incorporate it into one's own biography, to make it accessible to words. Everyday speech knows this condition which bespeaks speechless horror, the unthinkable, the ungraspable, although it makes use of it mostly for commonplace disturbances.

We are dealing here with events which are not mediated by the usual psychic process but are represented in somewhat singular fashion in the structure of the psyche itself. Neurobiological experiments have made it possible to reformulate these metaphors in medical terms. In situations of extreme stress, it can happen that mental impressions do not get transmitted to those parts of the brain that are designed to receive them as a precondition of their acceptance into the normal storehouse of memory. Nonetheless, they are preserved and can be called forth by any recurrence of stress, even much less severe stress. But they cannot be adequately verbalized, because the connection to the speech center of the brain remains disrupted.

This simultaneous occurrence of something terrifying that is both present and alien is the template of a classic literary form, the ghost story. It comes in two variants. In one, the ghost is a being that disappears ("is released") when it is recognized; it has made good on its previous sins, or whatever. In the other, which often tends toward the ordinary horror story, the ghost cannot be dealt with in this way. It must be destroyed (usually by main force). In the former case, the end result is something like the restoration of harmony; in the latter, even when there is a happy ending, the shadow of evil remains. In both types, the world is usually divided into a good side and a second side that breaks into it.

It is interesting how explicit a thought can become before you notice what it means. As he went up to his front door, he heard a rustling in the rhododendrons that grew to the right of the path. There were often animals in the shrubbery: mice, birds—and cats and weasels that knew there were birds or mice there. The rustling was too loud. He thought to himself: "That is more noise than a cat makes." The thought was complete, as if set in type—as if he had found it in his head and was reading it out loud: "That is more noise than a cat makes"—and then its metamorphosis into "and it's bigger than a cat" was already complete. Whatever it was, rustling in the bushes and making more noise than a cat, didn't belong there. If it had been a wild animal, the awareness of the noise and its consequence—a leap backward and immediate flight—would have been one single process, without any detour for articulated thought. So the only thing remaining is the memory of this peculiar, inconsequent sentence which had time to form itself in his head: "It's bigger than a cat."

I don't know how to put his fright into words. What happened was as conventional—a plot seen a hundred times on TV—as it was unreal and incomprehensible. The rhododendrons from which the rustling had come grew to the right of the door on top of a wall that was more than three feet high, and out of them came (sprang? no, it seemed so much slower than that) a masked man, above him, dropping at an angle toward him. He said to himself, again in words that were completely legible, "So it's happening," and yet was quite unsure about *what* was happening, for this sight could mean so many different things. A burglar, who wanted to force the householder to open first the door and then the (nonexistent) safe? Who was attacking him? The man now standing in front of him was tall, broad-shouldered, about the same height as he was, perhaps taller—I don't know, all I still see in front of me is a black mask covering everything except the eyes, like the terrorists in the Harrison Ford movie *Patriot Games.*

The last yards in front of his door were like a trap. The approach was narrow, with hip-high walls to right and left; to the left behind the wall the land falls away about six feet, to the right were the rhododendrons. He would have had to be very agile, athletic, and mentally alert to save himself by taking a leap to the left, and he was none of these things; to spin around and run was impossible. He attacked.

He had often thought about it. What can I do if someone attacks me? I'm probably going to lose anyway; the last time I fought anyone was in the school-yard when I was twelve. I can only win or somehow come out of it okay if I cause more pain or fright than the person who is attacking me expects. Because he had no experience in self-defense, all his thinking about it had been somewhat theoretical: when someone is attacking you, he needs both hands and cannot protect his face. If I can hurt the attacker's eyes, I may have a chance. So he went for the attacker, tried to stick both thumbs into the masked man's eyes, determined to retain the impulse to give no quarter and to render him truly unable to fight, to wound him, as painfully as possible. I think the masked man yelled, I am reasonably sure that he himself screamed, but perhaps it all happened silently. His right thumb was at the masked man's left eye, but was snared in the mask close to the lower eyelid; perhaps his inhibition about pushing the thumb through the eye into the head was too strong, or perhaps it was just the blow to his head that forced him around, but he fell to his knees, his glasses flew onto the paving (and with the noise came his fully formulated intellectual's decision to give up), someone (a second man had appeared out of the bushes, and became visible to him although he didn't actually see him) seized his head and slammed it into the wall.

When he had a conversation about these first few seconds with the one kidnapper to whom he occasionally had the opportunity to speak (and in English, which is why he thought of him as "the Englishman") in the thirty-three days that were to follow, the man said quite casually, "Well, now I can tell you, normally that would have been a deadly mistake. You tore his mask and you saw his face." He could not remember this but immediately said he had, and the kidnapper, with the coolness of an expert, replied that that didn't matter anymore: "People in shock don't remember things precisely, and he's far away now." I don't know whether the Englishman added that the attacker had only been hired for this one job, or whether that was something he himself had made up at the time.

It was about 8:30 p.m. It should have been a short, peaceful evening. The next day he wanted to be finished with his lecture, and wanted to be at his desk by 7:30. He intended to go to bed early, had drunk a bottle of red wine to make sure that he was ready for bed. Now he wanted to fetch a book. Had he only tried to defend himself because he had had the wine to drink? The Englishman seemed to think this was so, or so he said to him later. But that seems to indicate only how little they had expected he would defend himself at all. He had defended himself because he could not pass up his chances, given that he had some, and thus had done exactly what he had thought he would do in such a moment.

Looked at from a distance, his attempt at self-defense had been not only incredibly dangerous but also laughable. If he had surrendered at once, he would have avoided a broken nose and several damaged teeth. But still I do not regret that he defended himself; on the contrary. He did not allow himself to be simply rounded up before the front door by people who imagined that the moment he saw a black mask, he would give up. He tried to wound the attacker. He did not succeed, and I regret that.

Besides that, he had spoiled the image of a clear, professional (so to speak) abduction for the perpetrators. The unmistakable pool of blood in front of his door was a visible contradiction of the statement that often came later: "It's just business." And they—or at least the Englishman—wanted to keep rubbing that in: "If things had gone our way and you had cooperated, we wouldn't have had to break your nose." Was this already the prelude to the speech for the defense? A perfidious one, and fundamentally perverse: one avoids the most grisly variant of an act and takes credit for all "deviations below the norm" as mitigating circumstances. And if the act still doesn't fit the promulgated ideal, it's someone else's fault. Thirty-three days chained in the cellar? Yes, well, the police should have been more cautious, and the money carriers should have been better at it. And in explanation for having beaten him up, at least the people who had done the beating could say: If only he hadn't put up a fight!

When his head was slammed into the wall, he saw a flash of light, something like the drawing of an explosion in a comic book, star-shaped, notched, colorful, brilliant, not at all harsh. No pain. He wasn't surprised by this; a sentence came to him, that he had once read in Jean Améry: "The blow acts as its own anesthetic." Which made him wonder why they hadn't slammed his head harder against the wall. They could have broken his skull. His muscles went slack after the blow to the head, his power of self-defense had vanished. Granted, they didn't want to kill him, they wanted him as an object of live exchange, but at that moment he didn't know that. "They could have hit me harder" was the next sentence that went through his mind, which he registered in such a way that he was almost nonplussed.

He was yanked to his feet, heard: "You no fight back, nothing happens!" stammered, "All right, all right, what do you want?" and then they were already wrapping some kind of adhesive strip around his head to cover his eyes (not very carefully, however, he could see downward and he could have won any prize at pin-the-tail-on-the-donkey), another adhesive strip across his mouth. He couldn't breathe anymore. The blow against the wall had made his nose swell up within seconds. This wasn't clear to him at the time. It only became comprehensible later, when it took so many days for the swelling to go down again, and he didn't experience it as a problem, more as a physical confirmation of an otherwise incomprehensible fact, that he had been struck clean out of his life. But at that moment he had the panicked fear that he was going to suffocate, tried to say, "(I can't) breathe—air, air," until one of them opened his mouth, made a passage with a gloved hand between his lower lip and the adhesive bandage, and let him breathe. They handcuffed his hands behind his back.

A week after his release—miles away from Hamburg—I tried to make this scene real to myself by writing it down, and it turned out more or less as it appears here. I then immediately continued: "It's all so far away. Moments that still carry the label 'unforgettable,' like moments during a holiday recaptured when you look at a slide. I don't know what I feel anymore. But I still know the sentences that were in my head, and I would like not to neglect them as aids to reconstructing things. This time it wasn't a sentence that resurfaced involuntarily but something that I consciously said to myself: 'This is it now' and 'This is reality.' I said this to myself urgently and in silence, because I naturally could not, would not, believe it. 'THIS could not be. THIS (whatever it was, whatever it would demonstrate itself to be) was not a random something that could have been an identifiable rarity, it was no some-sort-of-thing, it was THIS, and the only thing I knew about it was that THIS should not be, ever, anywhere, should not have been, should not have been allowed to be. It was just there, and its actuality was the measure of how much I must convince myself, as I was thrust against the wall, led through the garden, shoved into the car, that THIS was reality, reality and nothing but, and most of all that nothing else was real for me anymore.'" This needs to be corrected, to say that returning to the scene of the crime—the front door, the rhododendrons, the blood that had soaked into the stone, and that heavy rains had not succeeded in washing away—brought the feelings back. The sound of a dog in the shrubbery has the effect of a memory that makes me feel ill for a moment.

As said before, they had failed to glue his eyes fully shut. He could see downward and, because the path sloped away, a little in front of him. He saw that the man in front of him was carrying something that he would have called a semiautomatic, but that experts call a "Kalashnikov" or just a "weapon," as I later had to learn. Even the Kalashnikov, appropriately, looked unreal, a film prop, precisely because the shape of this object is so well known. It was five weeks before I marveled at the audacity of the kidnappers. It wasn't even nine o'clock at night, they bound him and led him, carrying their Kalashnikovs in front of them, not just through his garden but out through an unlocked door, through a park in which around this time you could expect to stumble across people of all sorts taking a stroll, and dog owners on their evening rounds. But no one saw the three of them. They covered their route, which took somewhere between five and eight minutes, briskly but certainly not fast. The man with the Kalashnikov in front, the other one leading him by the right arm and his hands manacled at his back. They didn't push him forward. He tried to walk as if he couldn't see anything. When he stumbled, it was not met, as might have been expected, with "Faster, faster," or impatient twisting of the handcuffs.

He was grateful for the latter. The handcuffs were cutting into his wrists, particularly painfully against his right hand. There is no reason to assume this was intentional. In the haste of the attack, they had been put on wrong; they pressed immediately above the right wrist both up the arm and around it, rubbed one side raw and bleeding and on the other side pinched a nerve, with the result that his right thumb—from the ball to the tip—stayed numb for months.

On the journey to the hideout in which he was to spend the next thirty-three days, he asked repeatedly for the handcuffs to be loosened, but this was either ignored or not understood.

During the journey, he wondered what kind of an attack this could be—an attempt to extort money or something political, or a combination of both? He briefly weighed the possibility of a political assassination. The institute, which he had founded more than ten years ago and which he headed, had made headlines with an exhibition about the crimes of the German Wehrmacht, unleashing politically motivated controversy. The extreme right-wing press was full of language like "fouling their nests," and both he and other members of the institute had received letters saying that the institute was sullying the honor of German soldiers. But none of this fitted with the style of the attack or with the way he was being led away. They could have shot him in front of his house. If they wanted to subject him to a ritual trial somewhere to be followed by an execution, they would have handled him more brutally.

They came to a halt above the road that left the Elbe to head up the hill. He heard a car coming and thought they wanted it to pass, but the car stopped. A few yards down the slope, then they were on the road, he had to climb in through some sort of tailgate or flap and lie down. Then they drove off.

He had been able to see a little. It was a van, something like a small delivery truck, pale gray, as far as I can remember, the license plate was black on yellow, the first two letters FV or VF. "Vir Ferox" was the crib he gave it; a few hours before, he had been doing Latin vocabulary with his son.

Something was shoved under his head; he couldn't figure out what it was, something like a bedroll in a plastic cover, or perhaps a rolled-up tent. Perhaps even the thigh of one of the three men—but that was unlikely. There must be three of them in all, and he assumed from this that all three were sitting in the car, although of course he couldn't be sure. Someone was smoking, probably relieved that this part of the enterprise had been successfully concluded. After a few minutes it occurred to him that he should pay attention to the various parts of the route; that was how it always was in this sort of film—the people who'd been kidnapped made a mental note of their route—but they had already gone about two miles, and he didn't have a starting point from which to reconstruct things. If he could have done so at all. Thoughts were whirling in his head, and he had to keep telling himself: This is reality, this is really happening.

Fear gave way to a general despair as the thought came to him that perhaps his wife would go looking for him sometime in the night. When would her suspicions be aroused? When would the suspicion become certainty? How would she tell our son? And these thoughts kept being pushed aside again by the stabbing pains in his right wrist and the cramps caused by the position he was lying in. At some point he tried to turn over, and they let him do it. That way he was able to redistribute the pain to different parts of his body two or three times during the journey, only the pain in his right wrist could not be eased.

It is not easy to measure time in such circumstances, plus they removed his watch as soon as they arrived so that he would lose all sense of time. He did indeed lose it at once, but he had naturally noticed—quite independently from his later intuitive awareness of the passage of time—how long the trip had lasted when it came to an end. It had certainly lasted more than a half hour but less than an hour. Later it transpired that this memory had been inaccurate. In his shock, he had not been properly aware of the first phase of the journey before the entrance to the highway, and it was not part of his calculation of time. He had underestimated the second part. They had in fact traveled for about an hour and a half. Later he read that people in a state of fear who are locked up or trapped somewhere and cannot move tend to underestimate the time they have to spend wherever they are. Because every minute seems like an hour to them, they unconsciously overcompensate by shortening the time too much in their memories. They hardly ever stopped—if at all. I don't know anymore. He could not make out any lights or changing lights. If he could indeed see, or half see, half guess, there was a light on in the van, and the constant illumination led him to conclude that the rear part of the van had no windows, or had ones that were blacked out.

For most of the time they were traveling on a highway. At one point he almost thought he had lost his mind: he had the impression that the van was not moving under its own power but was being carried on the flatbed platform of a freight car. A regular clacking sound made him think of a train journey. He forced himself to admit that this must be impossible: if the van had been loaded onto a freight car, he would have had to notice this. Days later it dawned on him that certain old highway surfaces can produce a noise like that. There were some, or so he thought he remembered, on the highway from Hamburg to Bremen, but then they would have had to go through the Elbe tunnel and the change of sounds this would have engendered could not have escaped him. (They had gone through the tunnel. The road surface that had made the sounds had come right after the Elbe tunnel.)

Exit from the highway. A short stretch of country road, or so it seemed to him, then a side road. The light went out. Stop. The door was opened, he was allowed to get out. Commands such as "Out" or "Get out"? I cannot remember. They went into a house, one step up. An inner room, light on, a door, the stairs down. Wooden steps. He closed his eyes. He was afraid they would notice that he could see a little if he set his feet down too securely or anticipated changes of direction. The stairs made a half turn. He pretended he hadn't noticed, and allowed himself to be led. A door. A room. He opened his eyes again and saw a mattress on the floor, and a chain fastened to the wall. The handcuffs were unlocked and taken off. They removed his jacket, sweater, shirt, and trousers. They were all still masked but he saw one of them: short, light hair sticking out from the edge of the mask. He was allowed to keep his underpants. He realized they were not trying to humiliate him, and was relieved. His shoes were taken off, he was allowed to keep his socks. His watch and reading glasses, along with their case, were removed. Something like a sweater and a pair of trousers were put on him—later he saw that it was a gray sweat suit with red letters. He was made to sit in a chair, the chain was passed around his right ankle and closed with a small padlock. One of them took the adhesive bandage off his mouth and undid part of the other over his eyes. They somehow indicated to him that he could remove the rest when he was alone. I can no longer remember the words, only that it was something like "You not fight. Fighting Mafia." Whether this was supposed to mean that any form of resistance was pointless because he was in the hands of the (or a?) Mafia, or that it was only in Mafia films that a victim tried to defend himself in such circumstances, he couldn't say, nor could he identify either the unpleasantly aphoristic style of speech or the accent. Nonetheless, a general geographical conclusion of Eastern Europe seemed a good guess, but again this could have been prompted by press slogans like "Russian Mafia."

The door was closed. He pulled the adhesive bandage off his head and looked himself over: left hand covered in blood (at first he thought of the handcuffs, but it came from his face), the chain on his right foot. He looked around: a whitewashed room, about ten feet by thirteen, low-ceilinged, not even seven feet, certainly a cellar room, two windows boarded up, a table, a chair, both of them plastic, dark gray-blue, a foam rubber mattress with a sheet and covers (pale blue), a camping toilet, a wastepaper basket, a plastic bowl with water, a radiator next to the door, with a layer of chipboard. Right above the floor, an opening about a foot wide cut into the door, through which an invisible but very audible rush of air was being blown into the room. In the ceiling, a naked bulb, not switched on. On the table, bottles of water (Evian), two camp lanterns, one of them the only source of light, cardboard plate, plastic cutlery, a plastic sponge, toothbrush and toothpaste (Pearl White), soap (Fa— "the wild freshness" was the inappropriate slogan), toilet paper, writing paper, a ballpoint pen, a typewritten sheet, and instructions for using the toilet. One pair of glasses had been knocked off his head, and they had confiscated his reading glasses. He could hardly read the typewritten notice, and the printed instructions not at all.

The notice from the kidnappers was written in capital letters on what appeared to be an electric typewriter. He absorbed the text almost word for word, including the noticeable errors:

WE HAVE ABDUCTED YOU AND DEMAND
A RANSOM OF 20,000,000 FOR YOUR
RELEASE
THE MORE YOU COOPERATE WITH US
THE SOONER YOU WILL BE FREE AGAIN
DO NOT TRY TO ESCAPE BECAUSE IT IS
POINTLESS AND WOULD MAKE THE

CONDITIONS OF YOUR IMPRISONMENT UNBEARABLE
WRITE DOWN THE NAMES AND PHONE NUMBERS
WHICH ARE IMPORTANT FOR US
    RELATIVES
    CARETAKER
    TRUSTEES
YOU WILL GET FOOD IN THE MORNINGS AND EVENINGS
AT THOSE TIMES YOU CAN GIVE WRITTEN
MESSAGES AND REQUESTS
TO PREVENT SUICIDE
WE HAVE SHUT OFF THE LIGHT
WHEN WE KNOCK ON THE DOOR
LIE DOWN ON YOUR STOMACH WITH HEAD
ON THE MATTRESS!!!
ONLY USE THE TOILET FOR FECES!!!

That was more or less the letter. The exclamation marks were scattered about, but the last two sentences were exactly as they appear here. Apart from these, there were no punctuation marks. Minus his glasses, he could half read, half guess the sentences. Next he washed himself; the water was lukewarm and immediately turned bright red. He hadn't realized there was so much blood on him.

He was desperately afraid and at the same time relieved. IT had happened, but now he knew what IT was. An abduction. His life was in danger, but there was a chance he would survive this. At least they would keep him alive for the moment, they needed information from him, they would use him to write letters, someone whose continued existence would have to be proved over and over again. The kidnappers seemed to know what they were doing, an escape was certainly impossible, on the other hand they had provided fresh air for the cellar and he had water. They didn't want him to suffer hygienically, either. The sum of money also indicated perpetrators with a plan. After Richard Oetker's kidnapping, he had read that any amount over twenty million in thousand-mark bills made for transport problems.

But: when would his abduction be noticed? What were his actual chances of surviving IT? Criminal professionalism doesn't imply a disinclination to murder. For the moment he was worth twenty million marks, but if everything went according to the kidnappers' plan, he would soon be worth nothing anymore, and just be a possibly dangerous witness. One way or the other: how long was all this going to go on? If at some point they let him go, what kind of mental and spiritual shape was he going to be in? He would come to know these gusts of feeling, learn to live not with them so much as in them, but at the moment everything was too disorderly, too chaotic, not to mention unreal, so that he had to keep saying to himself that this is REALITY and certainly not some practical joke by some TV crew who would suddenly come through the door and yell "Fooled you!" On the other hand, reality could have had other things in store for him. He could have been dead already. He could have fallen into the hands of sadists who in addition to having a financial interest could have taken pleasure in torturing him. ANYTHING was possible. They could have bound him hand and foot. They could have kept him in pitch-darkness. He had light. He had been allowed to keep his underpants. The tone of the message was threatening but factual, and the threat about the change in the conditions of his imprisonment allowed him to hope that its present conditions would be continued, in order to be able to maintain the threat, which he took seriously and had no intention of testing to see if it would really be carried out or not. He sat down and wrote out the names and telephone numbers of his wife and his office. Then, on another piece of paper, that he needed his reading glasses, that he had only been able to read their message with some difficulty, and could not read the instructions for the toilet at all. And probably also (I don't know any longer) a request for something to read.

It was now somewhere around eleven o'clock at night. At some point he had to sleep; what would tomorrow be, what kind of a day would tomorrow be, would there be a tomorrow—and so on. He could not lie down as he had thought he could because the chain was too short. He put the pillow at the foot of the mattress.

He thought of his wife. When would she notice that something was wrong? He had said that he would be right back, but it happened sometimes that he stayed on longer in his work-house. He tried to concentrate his thoughts: "Go over, go over!" What would she find in front of his door? His glasses? Or had the kidnappers brought them along? That would indicate prudence and professionalism. That's what he should be hoping for. But if his wife were to find his glasses in front of the door, she would know exactly what had happened. How would she tell his son? He told himself not to cry. He would have done so gladly, but was afraid he would somehow be swept away by his own tears and would not be able to put the necessary face on things anymore. He had no idea what he could expect of himself. He literally did not trust himself very much. He had never felt himself to be a hero and knew that he would not become one. Nor, if everything went smoothly, would he be put to the test: to be a hero or a coward. (He still hadn't learned how much help a little heroism—even if imaginary—can be and how demoralizing the endless waiting in total passivity.)

He suddenly realized that he had no idea where he was. He didn't even know in what direction of the compass they had come. When does it ever happen that you have absolutely no idea of what part of a country you are in? That everyone who would be thinking about him in the next few days would be unable to connect their thoughts with any particular place. He had simply gone. Gone. When his son was little, he had said "go down" for "fall down." It was always said quite emphatically. "Oh, gone down!" Now he, his father, had somehow "gone down." This feeling, even worse than the continual fear of death, was the feeling that dominated the next thirty-three days: having "gone down" somewhere off the face of the earth. I had often used the metaphor "fallen off the face of the earth" for things other people had had to go through, and now he was learning with unpleasant exactness that this metaphor contained the precise feeling that was to take possession of him from now on. The first time I had come across the image was in Sigmund Freud's treatise *Civilization and Its Discontents,* where Freud is discussing a certain feeling of being uplifted in the world that some people know and rank as being among the supreme feelings of happiness, an "oceanic feeling." "I cannot discover," writes Freud, "this 'oceanic' feeling in myself"; the only thing he can do is "to fall back on the ideational content which is most readily associated with the feeling. If I have understood my friend rightly [Freud is here referring to a letter he has just received], he means the same thing by it as the consolation offered by an original and somewhat eccentric dramatist to his hero who is facing a self-inflicted death: 'We cannot fall out of this world.' That is to say, it is a feeling of an indissoluble bond, of being one with the external world as a whole." The quotation within the quotation is from Grabbe's *Hannibal,* and its exact wording is: "Indeed, we shall not fall out of the world. We are in it once and for all." But I believe in fact it's one of those wandering quotations which do not have any one particular source, because the feeling to which they give expression, or in this case, to put it better, the wish that they articulate, is universal and the metaphor is intrinsic to it. It also occurs in a children's book that I often read to my son, Barbro Lindgren's *Wild Hans and His Dog.* The German text is by James Krüss, and it came to his mind in the cellar. Wild Hans flies on his stuffed dog along with all his other stuffed animals through the universe: "But during their flight the mouse—oh no—falls away from its friends. They call, they ask, 'What's to be done, will it fall into bottomless nothing?' Then Wild Hans says, 'This dear little fat mouse is always falling out of something/Why not off a dog too? Calm down and wait till it finishes falling, for no one ever falls into nowhere AND NOTHING FALLS OUT OF THE WORLD.'" The consoling sayings of this world are the hollow shapes that are the surviving evidence of our anxieties. He had suddenly fallen out of the world. More precisely—had been struck out of it.

He fell asleep. Later he would lie awake for whole nights, but on this first evening he soon went to sleep—out of exhaustion and the desire to escape the consciousness of his situation. "A mixture of fear and weariness is the strongest sleeping pill," I read later in a book by Louis Begley. It's true. I do not remember if he dreamed. In later nights there were sometimes dreams, almost all of them friendly. None of them mirrored what had happened. One of them dealt with a kidnapping, but in it he was able to escape and even free other people. No triumphalism in this dream, just a peaceful transposition of a wish. His unconscious was friendly to him, just as his body was. He didn't catch cold, although the ventilator blasted uninterruptedly straight into his face from the slit at the foot of the door whenever he lay on the mattress. He positioned the washbasin so that it acted as a kind of regulator for the incoming stream of cold air. Anxiety attacks did not overly upset his stomach.

He awakened often in the night. It was darker in this cellar than all darknesses he had ever known before. It was utterly dark. There was not the faintest beam of light from anywhere, and it stayed that way whenever he turned off the artificial light, night or day. What he was unprepared for: this darkness was suffocating. It pressed on him physically. The only word I can use to describe it is *fat*. He had difficulty breathing, had the feeling he was drowning, a need to strike out. Luckily he had placed one of the camp lanterns within reach. With the light, the panic receded. He fell asleep again; woke again; fell asleep once more.

The next morning there was a knocking, and his insides cramped with fear, but it only announced the beginning of what he would come to know as a daily ritual: he lay, as ordered, with his face pressed into the mattress, his hands to the left and right of his head ("ready for a shot in the back of the head" was the thought that came to him), the door was opened, footsteps, something was set on the table, footsteps, someone removed the washbasin, the door was closed; a short time later more knocking, the basin was brought in again, filled with fresh water. And his written requests were taken away. This first time he heard the word "glasses" (it sounded as if it was being read out by someone who didn't speak good German), and with the washbasin came both pairs of glasses. And a copy of Monday's *Spiegel*.

The things that can go through one's head. He congratulated himself on having done no more than flip through *Spiegel* last Monday (he had had no time to read it, since he had to work on his speech). Then his glasses. They had brought them along—that meant he had left no traces (he knew nothing about the kidnappers' letter, the hand grenade, the overturned statue, nor how much blood he had lost). Last night's observation was confirmed: he had fallen into the hands of people who were self-assured, and this was primarily an advantage. (Later it turned out that this self-assurance was only partially an expression of their professionalism, the other part being hubris and stupidity. Lucky that he didn't know this in the cellar.)

When this account of the thirty-three days needs this or that revision (which are certainly pretty meaningless for the reader), it is because the utter uneventfulness, interspersed with shocks, the unaltering, empty time pierced with splinters of the drama which was meantime playing itself out elsewhere, makes it extraordinarily difficult to master chronologically. He asked repeatedly for his watch to be returned, and it was as a result of one of those requests that he was asked, "Do you speak English?" "Yes of course"—and so the conversations in the cellar all took place in English. The voice of the Englishman was accent-free, as far as he could tell, did not sound like that of a German speaking English, but like that of someone who has lived in England a long time. At some point, much later on, when the carpet was full of dust balls and he didn't want to see either himself or this hole of a cellar get completely filthy, he asked (in English) for a vacuum cleaner or at least a stiff brush. The Englishman answered: "Tomorrow, we'll get you a Hoover." A

Hoover. "Very idiomatic" is what his old English teacher would have said. Someone with good English but no particular idiomatic fluency would have repeated the textbook "vacuum cleaner."

So this English voice told him that he'd have his watch back in two days; "You have to lose your sense of time." How illuminating. And what a vast lack of information such a sentence contains. First: the repeated assertion that you are in the power of people who somehow know what they are doing, at least in a technical sense. A source of some comfort. Second: they haven't thought it out *that* well, since loss of a sense of time would only confuse your memory of how much time had actually elapsed if this were to lodge in your mind as pure feeling and not as a calculated formula. Taking his watch away has no effect on the sentence he had memorized: "It was longer than a half hour and less than an hour" (the fact that he had only a vague sense of time during his actual abduction is a separate matter). Third: the connected thought that if they want me to be unable to give any information about the length of the journey, they are not going to kill me. But fourth: what about the return journey? He would certainly be able to measure *that* time if they gave him back his watch later. Here his thoughts jammed. So why the theatrics over the confiscation of his watch? It seemed to him only to make sense as a way of preventing him from inserting some secret message in one of the notes he would have to write, or, not unrelated, to suggest to him that they were going to release him, whereas in fact they intended to kill him, because otherwise they would never give him back the watch at all. For a time this conclusion struck him as compelling. Then he wondered if they wanted to confuse him about the duration of his overall stay in the cellar, if perhaps they wanted to say that three days had gone by when in fact it was only two, or if they could gain some advantage if they reversed day and night, let him sleep all day and brought him breakfast in the evening. Then he hit upon a quite simple explanation: they would take him home by a different route. Remarkably, he never considered what did eventually happen. A day before he was released, they took his watch away again and did not return it after they set him free, so he went through the journey in the trunk of the car and then the walk through the woods with an impaired sense of time, and knew only what time it was when he arrived. Writing all this down, like certain other things, is a curious experience. I still know how the question of the confiscated watch kept turning in his mind, how much he tried to make it the oracle of his survival, and I cannot reconstruct either his thoughts or his feelings about it. At this point I only know that he spent days worrying at this problem. I am confronted with the hysterical foolishness of a man I was for a time, and whose nerves were in quite bad shape.

The actual circumstance of having no watch is different. He would get his watch back the next day, or perhaps two days later, "but it won't help you much." As if the Englishman knew what he was talking about. Perhaps he did from long periods in prison. I know how *much* a watch helps. You distribute the day and with it the problem that confronts you and consists of nothing more than a confrontation with time itself. You apportion. From ———— to ———— I will do this, then that. You can focus your inner resources and conquer one hour after the other. Without a watch you are in a sea of time, out of sight of land. No, worse, in a barrel whose sides are too high and give no purchase. You will keep swimming for as long as your strength holds out, knowing all the time that you aren't going anywhere and that sooner or later you will drown.

For example, the time between 5 p.m. and 8 p.m. was unnaturally long. It felt as if hours had gone by, and they were only quarter hours. Without a watch, another disproportionate panic would have been inevitable; with a watch, the phenomenon was the infinite elasticity of time. With a watch, you do not rule time, but it does not rule you, either. It becomes neutral, the external world, a problem. Without a watch, at bottom, there is no time, only eternity; you are cast into eternity, and eternity is utter standstill. The words may seem to be reaching too far for two days without a watch, but the intensification of the reality of being abducted and of the complete loss of certainty brought on by the simple act of removing the watch is worth commenting on.

When he got the watch back, he wrote a note of thanks and confirmed: "You were right. It doesn't help much." The truth is somewhat other, but he wanted at all costs to neutralize the watch as a possible weapon of sanction. (In retrospect, these are idle reasonings, but at the time they seemed much more important than a great deal else.) In *The Bonfire of the Vanities*, a copy of which he was given later, he read this about the arrest and temporary detention of a civilized man. "'Yeah, you can keep it [a handkerchief]. But you gotta give me the watch.' 'It's only—it's just a cheap watch,' said Sherman. . . . [He] undid the band and surrendered the little watch. A new spasm of panic went through him. 'Please,' said Sherman. As soon as the word left his mouth, he knew he shouldn't have said it. He was begging. 'How can I figure—can't I keep the watch?' 'You got an appointment or something?'" But the watch is not only a symbol of civilization, although it is that. It is one of the tools that allows you to maintain contact with the world.

But back to the chronology. A knock on the door. He was told to stand up. I no longer remember whether words were uttered or whether he was pulled off the mattress to his feet. (So much for the exact memory of the victim.) Without being ordered to, he kept his eyes shut. Whether they expected this of him, I do not know; he assumed it was an order. He didn't know what was coming next. He had to sit on the chair, paper was put into his hand. An inner picture flashed: Schleyer.* It was a newspaper. He couldn't stop himself from giving voice to his thought: "Oh, that!" He sat, held the paper spread in both hands. A flash, the

---

*Hans Martin Schleyer, chairman of the German Employers' Association, kidnapped and killed by the Red Army Faction. There exists a famous photograph of him, taken by his kidnappers, in which he is holding up a newspaper.

sound of a Polaroid camera, another flash, the sound of the picture sticking its tongue out at the object it had just photographed, and he certainly didn't want to look at it. So he saw neither the apparently masked photographer nor the man, also apparently masked, standing next to him pointing the Kalashnikov at him. He had no idea how the picture looked.

They left him the *Bild Zeitung* with the headline "Look How Happy We Are!" and the photo of Gerhard Schröder, Premier of Lower Saxony and his new love, an editor of *Focus*. They left *Focus,* too. Now he had three newspapers. He remembered what a former colleague at the Hamburg Institute for Social Research had told him about his time under deportation arrest: "Then quite by chance I found a newspaper. That's when I broke the record for slow reading." A few months previously I had been invited to do a critique of *Spiegel* by the editors of the magazine. In preparation for it I had read *Spiegel* from cover to cover, and found it indigestible, but now he read every word including the advertisements. The devil will eat flies when he has to, as the saying goes, or, he ate the whole pig, down to the "oink." Amazing, incidentally, how many ads *Spiegel* carries for building materials. What conclusions can be drawn from this about their readership or what their advertisers believe to be their readership? He had so much time. What an expert report lost to mankind: "The *Spiegel* reader. A profile drawn from the analysis of those who desire him as a customer." (Such jokes would never have come to his mind in the cellar. He remembered how often he had used to laugh, because there was one single time when he almost did laugh now, while reading a "Spotlight" column in the *Süddeutsche Zeitung* about politicians only pretending to eat in public—mad cow disease was all over the papers at the time. Thanks to whoever wrote that one!)

They also left him written instructions to write a letter and instigate the assembling of the ransom payment. He set about it immediately. He addressed the letter to his wife, the head of his Hamburg office, and his lawyer.

Dear Kathrin,
Dear Mr Fritzenwalder,
Dear Joachim,
I have been abducted. The ransom demand is for 20,000,000 Deutsche marks (twenty million). Please pay the money and hand it over according to their demands. Given the circumstances, I am fine. Please do everything to ensure that I come out of this soon.
Jan Philipp Reemtsma

P.S. Dear Kathrin, dear Johann—I love you. Hold yourselves together—I will too—promise.
Your F.

Then he began to wait. Nothing happened. They did not fetch the letter. Time passed, he couldn't measure it. He made bets: I made a mistake, it's only been about two hours, when his instinct told him it was already five. He read the words in *Spiegel* one after the other, every word of every advertisement, he even went over the page numbers, he walked up and down, counted his steps, also the amount of time he had used up. At some point it became almost impossible to read anymore, because one of the two camping lanterns was no longer giving enough light. He turned the other on. Read, walked, waited. It was not just the undifferentiated time which would not pass, but his steadily increasing, noticeable, and real anxiety: why don't they collect the letter? There is *no* reason not to. They have every reason to speed things along, and if they don't collect the letter, it's because there's a reason, which could be that the whole affair has become too hot for them; they really are amateurs, some collection of wannabes, and they've lost their nerve (how close his anxiety of that time was to reality became clear later); they've cleared off and I'm sitting here chained in a cellar and at some point the light is going to give out. Then all I can do is try to scratch out the dowelling that is fastening the chain into the wall, using the plastic cutlery. It won't work. (But if it does work, can I use the dowelling to loosen the planking over the windows? I can try making noise. Nobody will hear me. Well, perhaps. But if they *haven't* left, how will they carry out their threat that "the conditions of my imprisonment will become unbearable"? Handcuffs, gags, etc.? The threat worked: he made no attempt to free himself. He waited, read, walked up and down. The second lamp began to dim. The various possibilities he was considering narrowed to a single foreseeable reality: the light was going to go out. If he was going to have to rot here, soon he would no longer have any chance to leave a letter behind. If it came to that, he wanted some words to be found with his body, addressed to the two people he loved. As he wrote, he noticed that the text helped him reassert some measure of self-control. The fear did not leave him, but he rediscovered himself as a human being.

Dear Kathrin,
Dear Johann,
I don't know what is going to happen, but most of all I don't know how much longer I will have light to write. I have heard nothing from my abductors for ? hours, a letter I wrote, Kathrin, to you, Joachim, and Mr. Fritzenwalder has not been collected. In the worst case, they will leave me behind here—wherever that is—and then I'll be like Indian Joe in Tom Sawyer. *But again, perhaps not, and everything will be fine. We'll see. I just want to tell you both how much I love you, and that I think back on every moment in our lives together with love and happiness. No matter what happens, I have had a wonderful life—Thank you both.*
Your Jan Philipp

A farewell letter, composed to be found at some point next to the corpse. He folded it up and stuck it under one of the two lamps. Then he waited again.

I am transcribing this letter, trying to evaluate the frame of mind of the man who wrote it. I agree with it, it is not a pose, although it also simulates to some small degree the attitude he would want people to ascribe to him if they eventually found him. But it is also a method of assimilating that attitude. If I had to die today, I would write the same letter.

I have wondered for a long time whether I should avoid mention of the fact that this letter, which I intended to be the possible closure of my life, contained two hidden allusions. "Tell them that I've had a wonderful life" are the last words of Ludwig Wittgenstein, and "no matter what happens" is a leitmotif from the film *Rocky IV.* After my initial surprise, I realized that Wittgenstein's words—so different from his life—have always made it clear to me that when you look back you see that your life could not have run its course very differently and that it really wasn't so bad. It pleased him that in the face of the unexpected, the violent destruction of his life, he should cite this peaceful backward look—and use the both trivial and quite wonderful "I love you, no matter what happens" from *Rocky IV* to bring the requisite touch of irony to the proceedings. For—and I want to say this even at the risk of being thought unserious—if there is one essential to both life and survival, it is irony. You draw on it more than courage or even hope. The worst moments in the cellar were those in which he lost his resources of irony or had not yet recovered them. And Indian Joe? His death had always seemed a nightmare to me: to slowly waste away of thirst in a dark hole, unable to make a sound, spending days and days doing nothing but scratching at a door which there was no hope of opening or even damaging with a knife. Now there was some possibility that his own life would end in such a nightmare. He didn't want to write "I'll die of thirst here." He wanted to interpose the analogy between himself and a possible reality, to lend the latter a certain air of fiction, to push it out of his mind.

Sometime during the evening they came. In answer to the question of why the letter had not been collected, the only reply was "Wrong paper." Nothing more. What this meant, I do not know to this day—at the time he thought it must have something to do with the fax machine, since he had been told there would be no telephoning, only faxes. In the meantime, I have learned that there was one attempt to send a fax without a sender code, and that all further written communications came by mail. Probably the kidnappers had touched the paper and had to get a new supply. However that may be, the contrast between his feelings and the banality of the explanation was not only immense but shattering, because it was yet another clear demonstration of how dependent he had been on every mood and even the pure thoughtlessness of his abductors.

The Englishman took the letter nonetheless, and also discovered and removed the farewell letter from under the lamp. The next morning he was supposed to write both letters over again. That one of the two was no letter at all didn't occur either to his wife or to the police, and they attached the wildest interpretations to the *Tom Sawyer* reference, such as that he must be being held in a cave near the Elbe or in a former bunker. He was instructed to add a demand to the other recopied letter that the police should be left out of things. He added a second P.S.:

P.P.S. I have been informed that the police are undertaking a search for my hiding place. Any kind of search will only prolong matters. As previously stated, I am being well treated in the circumstances, but any act that brings this current state of affairs to an accelerated conclusion would be very welcome to me.
Kathrin, I love you (hug Johann, + he you), your F.
Jan Philipp Reemtsma
27:3:96

He paused at the word "search" (in the written instructions for this letter) because it could at most be a wide general search, not the sort of police work with full computer support that is usually implied by this word, but he wrote it down as instructed. Then he made another urgent request for reading matter. If they wanted him to remain clear-headed—so that he could write letters and provide information—they should give him things to read. A book, a thick one if possible, and he proposed the Bible. As he did not expect the kidnappers to undertake major book purchases for him, he wanted to suggest something that would be available even in smaller bookshops (he assumed he was somewhere in the country) and that if necessary could be stolen from any village church.

The next day after the knocking, entering, and leaving, he found a bag (Karstadt or Kaufhof) with the

Chronicle of the 20th Century and an illustrated book entitled *Paintings of the Prado*. At the same time, the bulb in the ceiling was restored to use, so that he could switch it on and off himself. It brought tears to his eyes and he felt bottomlessly grateful. I will deal with these feelings of gratitude toward his abductors more fully at a later juncture; here the point is merely to establish them. A day later, a further delivery of books, five titles: John Le Carré's *The Little Drummer Girl,* Tom Wolfe's *The Bonfire of the Vanities,* a little Suhrkamp volume on Peter Sloterdijk's *Critique of Cynical Reason,* Karl Jaspers's *The Great Philosophers,* and Dostoevsky's *Stories.* All in all a selection that amazed him. Someone had applied some real thought to this, even if amateurishly, and pulled together a really good mixture: a thriller, a novel, a classic, some philosophy. He was almost moved by the care. On the other hand, the number of books told him that the kidnappers were not expecting to get things over with in a day or two. As the affair was drawn out longer than the abductors had anticipated by two failed handovers of the money, he received two more deliveries of books. The second time they were also, he thought, quite carefully chosen, as can be seen from the titles: Karl Kraus's *Far and Near,* containing the draft of "Third Walpurgisnacht," Doris Lessing's *Going Home,* Simone de Beauvoir's *The Second Sex,* Ostrovsky's *The Other Side of Deception,* A. E. Johann's *The Silent Wilderness.* The last delivery by contrast seemed carelessly put together: Bruce Chatwin's *The Songlines; Childhood Happiness,* a gruesome anthology; and a collection of odds and ends, like Cronin's *Late Victory,* Kishon's *Picasso's Revenge,* Serge Filippini's *Man in Flames,* Sten Nadolny's *The God of Impertinence,* and *While the Pillars Still Stood,* a guide to Greece written after Pausanias. There has been a great deal of speculation about the books, perhaps all of it wrong. Even the first two deliveries after the *Chronicle* and the *Prado* could have been random selections: one from the Suhrkamp section, two from the Piper* shelf, etc. After his release I received a letter in which someone suggested that the books indicated a woman's choice. Not a stupid thought, not only because of the de Beauvoir but also because of the Le Carré and the Lessing. Always assuming that the person doing the choosing knew the books. One could just as well detect a preference for travel books (Lessing, A. E. Johann) or a particular interest in the Israeli secret service (Ostrovsky, Le Carré).

It is true that the Englishman had said "We won't use the phone," but the telephone numbers did play a role, after all, because both had recently been changed; the new ones were very close to the old ones, and in his determination to avoid confusing them, he at first got them completely mixed up. Then they wanted the plate number of his car and his wife's—he had to write them out. At first he thought this must be a question coming from home, to ascertain if he was still alive. He wrote with some irritation that they shouldn't ask him such stupid questions, since he

---

*Suhrkamp and Piper are both German publishers.

obviously could only give them an approximate idea. But it was the kidnappers who wanted to know the numbers so that they could identify the cars when the money was handed over. There was also one of the questions from the small ads in the *Morgenpost* that he had to answer sometime later in writing. I don't know if it played any part in the telephone communication.

One short conversation was devoted to the question of who should deliver the money. The abductors wanted it to be either his wife or his gardener, who had just retired but whom they knew from their surveillance of the property. He dissuaded them from the latter. Then they asked if his wife was strong enough to handle the money. Both physically and psychically. He said yes in both cases, but the question left him almost in despair; what was he doing saying yes? First and foremost: she would have to leave our son Johann alone in order to deliver the money. He hoped she would think up some solution. He could dream up nothing himself, and didn't feel that there would be any point in it even if he could. Moreover, he was still hoping that the thing could be over by the day after tomorrow—just as his wife was at that same time.

Then the Englishman let him read the announcement in the *Morgenpost,* prefacing it with something resembling a protective gesture: "Don't be afraid, everything is okay with your wife, it's just the police psychologist." It was the announcement "I am exhausted. Gerhard will do everything for me."

Who might Gerhard be? He knew only one Gerhard, Gerhard Schwenn, the partner of his lawyer

Joachim Kersten. Gerhard Schwenn had gone to school with him. His name was Gerhard Johann Schwenn; he had always called himself Gerhard back then, but then had switched his first names and his name appeared as Johann Schwenn even on the letterhead of the law firm. Why not use "Johann" in the announcement? Because his son's name was also Johann and a notice that said "Johann is doing everything for me" could only lead to misunderstandings. "Gerhard" would mean only one thing to him. Besides, he would find the idea an obvious one.

He had already been given the first announcement to read, and it had been a promise that this horror story would soon be over. He had placed it on the table where he could see it, and did the same with the next one he was given. At some point the sight just upset him, and he put them away.

He kept asking to be allowed to write letters, and also asked, in order not to make the letters a problem, if there was anything he shouldn't write. Laughter: "You can write what you know. . . ." It was little enough. So he described his living arrangements in the cellar. He wanted to calm his wife and son. Hygiene was taken care of, he was being given food and water, even things to read "even if—well, you know. . . ." He said nothing about the chain; he simply mentioned that he walked up and down in the cellar and had managed to get up to eighteen thousand strides in one day. This letter was not sent on, as he learned later. The Englishman soon told him that the kidnappers didn't approve of the letter, but he understood him to mean that at least parts of the letter had been sent on, with just the soothing passages cut out: "We have to put some pressure on them." As if that had been necessary. A subsequent letter passed the censors:

Dear Kathrin, dear Johann—I am allowed to write to you, but what can I write to you except that I wish I were with you! I love you, I know how hard all this is for you. Johann, we can do something together. Every day at 5 p.m. (I think "MacGyver" is over by then) we will each take the Chronicle of the 20th Century *and look up what happened on this day (date) between 1900 and 1995. We'll do it simultaneously. Today is March 30, and I'm beginning here. You will probably get this letter tomorrow at the earliest. See you soon, I hope. I hug you both and kiss you, Kathrin—Your F.*

P.S. Johann: Play "Boring" for me!

He assumed that his son's consumption of TV would be reaching lonely heights during this time, and he didn't want his suggestion to cut into his favorite program. He made this proposal in the hope that there would be only a few days more ahead of him. As time went on, it became harder each day to keep the 5 p.m. appointment. He always became almost physically nauseated from sadness, but he was too conscientious or perhaps too superstitious to break off the ritual. (His son only did it for the first few days, then intelligently kept his fingers out of it. What was a means in the first few hopeful days of establishing an emotional link soon became nothing but torture. In the cellar he hoped that his son would be smarter than he was—and yet also hoped the opposite, as a later letter will show.) The P.S. also led to an almost comic episode. "Boring" was a song by his son's favorite group, die Ärzte. In the letter that was held back, he had already asked his son to play this song for him and had mentioned the name of the group. "Are die Ärzte a band from Bremen?" he was asked. They thought he had been trying to pass a hidden message concerning his whereabouts. But that was quite unnecessary; in the photo of him anyone could have noticed that he was holding up a Bremen edition of *Bild Zeitung*. He had not noticed this, because he simply had not looked closely enough at the paper.

Since this time he kept thinking about how he could avoid writing something that might be construed as a hidden message, and came to the conclusion that it was unavoidable. A suspicion that information is concealed somewhere produces its own proof, since it cannot be refuted. In the event, you cannot reach a conclusion that there is no coded message in a text—all you can say is that you haven't found it yet.

But once he did send a letter that really did enclose a message, and he sent it with the knowledge and permission of his abductors. Information had emerged that there was unease because the police were working on the assumption that there was only one perpetrator. This didn't make sense, the police must have seen traces of two perpetrators. "But your wife told the police that if there had been more than one, you wouldn't have fought." That sounded so much like a verbatim quote that he had the impression the kidnappers were bugging police conversations. (In fact, a similar conversation had taken place, as he learned later. Although the police never assumed that there was only one perpetrator, they had naturally wanted to reconstruct the scene on the evening of the abduction and explain the traces of the struggle.)

This troubled him. To underestimate the kidnappers was a mistake from any standpoint. He said he would write. "They will think we forced you to write that." So he would build some information into a letter that they would understand at home, but that the Englishman would not understand without this information. The letter ran:

Dear Kathrin—how is life for you both these days? I think about it often—and then stop myself quickly. You must make decisions, and yet you don't know which are the right ones. I sit, lie, walk around, can do nothing: it is sometimes shaming, sometimes it makes me crazy, sometimes it is painful and yet calming. The whole story is enough to make you superstitious: the last thing I read at home was Dostoevsky's Notes from the Underground *for the lecture I should have been giving in St. Louis today, and a few days ago I was complaining about various boring things—so, here again is FAUST II. "And imaginary, the way it is" (I wish the lesson could have been avoided!). I love you—I wish I could see you again soon!*

Dear Johann—please give Kathrin a big hug and both of you think of me. *And say hello to our whole zoo—Cinnamon + Caraway + Currant—Benni + Franz + Fritz!*

Be well. Till soon, Your F.

"Here again is FAUST II." In the letter that unbeknownst to him had not been sent, he had quoted from the second part of *Faust*—"Two of mankind's greatest enemies/Fear and hope"—and recommended a "depressed middle position" as the ideal frame of mind for both himself and his family. (Whoever actually looks up the quotation will be able to see how the unconscious plays games.) But because this letter wasn't there to be read, the "here again" made no sense. But the letter still contained two pieces of information. First, that he was sitting in a cellar, and second, that there were at least three perpetrators who had him in their power, one of whom should be assumed to be guarding him at all times.* He hoped someone would notice. But this was the less important clue. He had worked the second into the text four times. Once via two (so he thought) very noticeable sequences of threes: "sit/lie/walk" and "shaming/crazy/calming." Then there was the underlined sentence; this hug was known in their family language from when Johann was very young as "Doing All Three." Lastly, he sent greetings to the three cats and three

---

*In German, the Dostoevsky novella is most often given the title *Notes from the Cellar.*

dogs, but there were only two dogs. The third, "Fritz," was an invention from their previous vacation, when he had gotten on his son's nerves by having conversations with an invisible dog named Fritz: sending greetings to a dog that only he could see was something of a contradiction of all the rules of this fantasy game, was a way of calling attention and drawing the eye toward the two three-word sequences. (As I later discovered, the only result was that this intentional mistake was taken to be an actual one, and was interpreted as an alarming indication of his mental state.) And finally, he had hidden the number in the Faust quote. He assumed that even if no one had the quote at their fingertips, someone would look it up or ask a Goethe expert. It might even have been possible, finally, that someone had read his book on the style of Muhammad Ali and would have remembered that the same quote was used in it as a motto. Whatever; it could have struck someone—*must* have struck someone, he thought—that the quotation was wrong. The correct version is "And imaginary as the scoundrels are," and the emphasis on the "scoundrels" by leaving them out had to be a sign of something relating to the situation they all found themselves in. The context would have revealed that the subject is "three mighty men"*— Grabber, Hoarder, and Quick—whom Mephistopheles summons to win the battle. Among other things the passage says, "When a man looks me in the eye/I promptly smack my fist into his mouth," then, "Be tire-

*Louis MacNeice translation of *Faust II*.

less raking in the spoils/Then you can ask for all the rest," and finally, "Taking is quite all right/It's better still to keep things." This all seemed to him quite allegorical enough. But the effort was pointless. Later I heard that everyone had had to admit that even in such a horrible situation he had had his *Faust* quotes ready. Which made him the only one. Luckily this letter was irrelevant.

Finally the transfer of the money was supposed to take place. He was told he might be able to be home by Easter. He was allowed to write again:

Dear Kathrin—This evening it will be a week since they seized me in front of my own door. I could hardly understand back then that this was real—and now for you both and for me, everyday reality is an absurdity that is no part of this world at all. I hope so much that we will be together again soon—do what you can so that they let me out [a second "out" was crossed out] of here—and soon!

Dear Johann—did we both look at the Chronicle *today at five o'clock? I did—stupid dates! (But nothing we can do about it.) I hope we're together again soon (and play—you know—for me).*

A hug

Your F.

And, commenting on the date, "April *1,* 96 (ha ha ha)."

What he meant by "stupid dates" I can no longer reconstruct. I seem to remember an entry about the first performance of an opera that had something about murder in the title, but can find no such entry in my current *Chronicle*. This could be due to a fault in my memory, or else it's a new edition. But perhaps what's meant is also the abduction of the German ambassador to Guatemala, Count von Spreti, on March 31, 1970; his body was found on April 5. (The *Chronicle* lists a remarkable number of kidnappings, as he could not fail to notice.)

On the morning of April 3 the Englishman arrived in the cellar, audibly angry: if things kept going like this, the affair would go on for months! Nobody had come. This was shattering not only because he had been hoping constantly that everything would soon be over (but always with the doubt about whether "over" meant freedom or death), but also because he did not understand what was happening in the outside world. Why had nobody come? An announcement in the *Morgenpost* of April 2 had asked for a fresh proof that he was alive. "Tell me, why haven't you sent me a picture?" Was that why they hadn't come? "Nonsense! They don't need a picture! You're writing letters, they know you're alive!" Besides, there were apparently police in the wood where they had waited. Had there been an attempt to strike at the kidnappers at the handover? They seemed to think so. He must write to his lawyer and make clear whose interests the latter was to represent—those of his client rather than those of the police. And then: "We told your wife we'll cut your finger off!"

The letters I am about to reproduce here are embarrassing to me. They show him in a state that is unfortunately a long way from what I previously called "maintaining face." If they were to be read aloud, it would have to be in a shrill voice. His wife said to him later that she had held these two letters against him somewhat. I can understand why. He had not made her situation easier; quite the opposite. To excuse him, I can only add that the prospect of possibly having to spend months in this cellar was terrifying to him—far more so than the threat about his finger, if he took it seriously at all. In addition, he had no idea what was going on, could make neither head nor tail of the fact that nobody had come to the rendezvous to hand over the money, except that his wife and his lawyer, for reasons he could not imagine, were following some plan proposed by the police, which had as its primary goal something other than his immediate release. On the other hand, he knew his wife and could not imagine that anything would be more important to her than getting him out of here. So what had happened? The kidnappers could have no possible interest in prolonging things.

Strictly speaking, these letters are proof that the abductors had persuaded him over onto their side a little. He had great difficulty ridding himself of the idea that his situation was not being taken seriously enough, that there were other considerations, other motives, other who-knew-what, playing a role over and above the goal of getting him free. These might all be plausible, but he wanted to get out of here, and nothing else should count, thank you very much!

Wednesday, April 3, 1996
Dear Kathrin—*I don't know what you're all doing, the handover of the money last night failed, nobody came. I'm afraid!* The atmosphere is radically *worse, they have threatened that this could go on for months and they will cut off one of my fingers. I do not consider these empty threats. Please, Kathrin, believe me and help me. Now! No more hesitations! You said Gerhard would take over everything, and since I don't know any other Gerhard, this must be* Gerhard Schwenn. *If it really is Gerhard and not someone from the police, I agree. I have described Gerhard. I will say something to the kidnappers* that only Gerhard will be able to answer, *so that he is* unequivocally identifiable. *Another possibility would be* Mr. Fritzenwalder. *He will have to answer a question, too.* Kathrin, give instructions that this is how things must be done. I love you! Help me, I'm afraid and I can't go on. It's got to happen tonight!
Jan Philipp

For identification (you don't need a picture of me, that would only hold things up!): The heading of the third section of today's Süddeutsche Zeitung *is "UN Report on Chechnya: Human Rights Are Being Trampled Underfoot," and "Searchlight" begins with "Karl, the son of the Germans."*
Jan Philipp

To Gerhard Schwenn
Wednesday 3.4.1966 [sic!]
Dear Gerhard—I assume from the announcement
that you will be making the handover of the money for
Kathrin. I agree and I thank you. But please do not let
this turn into some concealed police exercise *(or, like*
last night, nothing at all—why did nobody come??). I am
truly in great danger now! So please, hand over the
money tonight!! And if you don't want to do it, Mr.
Fritzenwalder will do it. *These are my* express instructions! *In each case I will give the kidnappers a question*
that only you or Mr. Fritzenwalder can answer so that
there is clear identification. Do as I say, no more police
tactics!
Jan Philipp Reemtsma

For identification, today's Süddeutsche Zeitung *right*
at the top "Lech Walesa—a colleague . . ."

The rudeness of the repeated exclamation marks
and underlinings shows the frame of mind he was in,
and the phrase "no more police tactics!" shows that he
had partially adopted the kidnappers' point of view.
That he was also rejecting the principle of avoiding
naming anyone whom he employed as a possible
money carrier shows the state of his nerves. Admittedly, this had been an idea of the kidnappers, but he
should not have gone along with it, and should have
made other suggestions instead. He did indeed ask
himself whether he had the right to say that he

couldn't go on anymore. But then he made the wrong decision. He was living, as previously stated, under the delusion that his situation was somehow being judged as relatively rosy. He was still proceeding under the assumption that his letter describing his living conditions had been received, at least in part, and wondered if he had painted too friendly a picture of the situation, so that people thought, for whatever reason, that another couple of days or so would be all right.

He miscopied the heading from the *Süddeutsche Zeitung*. He realized this just after the letter had been taken away. It didn't say "Trampled Underfoot"; it said "Trampled with Booted Feet." *That* would certainly be taken as a hidden message, to wit: Things not that bad by half! He wrote another P.S., banged furiously on the door, and when the Englishman came, pushed it out through the air vent.

Dear Kathrin—I was in such a state that I misquoted the Süddeutsche Zeitung. *It should be "Human Rights Are Being Trampled with Booted Feet," not "Underfoot."—This isn't a hidden message or some other piece of madness, just my state of nerves. Please hand the money over today.* I cannot go on.

Jan Philipp

Another identification from the Süddeutsche Zeitung: *The last heading in the left-hand corner (page 1) runs "Arafat: Plans for Referendum Endangering Peace Process."*

Again the unfortunate "I can't go on!" He had forgotten that he had just written this already. And yet
another identification using a newspaper heading,
quite unnecessary, shows how his nerves were even
worse than what is usually called "shot."

There is another, calmer aspect of the thing—and
one that is more distanced from the shame that I feel
on rereading this letter—that is not unimportant: at
the time he wrote it, he had not yet become accustomed to his imprisonment. That said, he never did
nor ever could have really adjusted to it, but the contrast between the first days and the last was immense,
and not just because they were the last, since he only
knew they were such in the final forty-eight hours. In
the first days, he asked the Englishman stupid questions such as: "Do you expect something tomorrow?"
"Expect what?"—the handover of the ransom money,
obviously. He did not understand why the event
should be taking so long. But the standard answer was
"This needs time."

When he heard before the first failed handover that
if everything went according to plan, things would last
another five days, the news hit him like a blow. When,
two weeks later, the handover in Luxembourg failed
and the abductors demanded neutral go-betweens, he
wrote in his diary that if everything went well next
time, he would have to prepare himself for another two
weeks. It was a grim prospect, and he wrote this as a
preventive measure so as to get used to the idea, but it
was nothing like as grim as the prospect of five days

had been more than a week before. Three things come together here. First, you have learned that you can in fact get through the low points of such days, something you don't yet know in the first few days. Second, you measure the length of a day in proportion to the way it relates to an entire period (which is why the first two weeks of a vacation are always so much longer than the last two weeks). Third, this space out beyond the world into which you have been thrust becomes its own world. Its walls become familiar. It becomes possible really to lose yourself in a book and not just use your reading as a hysterical way of passing the time. And so on. You can get used to anything, as people have said and written who have gone through much worse things than he. In any case, I would like to emphasize that the verb "get used to" does not have the comfortable echo in this context that it does in our everyday life, where it is whispered into the bedcovers with a small sigh as we open our eyes. In this context, "getting used to" means that unhappiness spreads inside, becomes part of you, that the chance you may surface from your unhappiness as if from a nightmare you can wash away under the morning shower steadily diminishes. "Getting used to" means a heightened pathogenic intensity: the soul plucks terror from its all-enveloping immediacy and makes it part of time, captures it from its free-floating otherness and makes it part of life. The strength you win is wrested from resources which you will no longer be able to draw on in future, and the gain lacks all proportion to the loss. Or does it? Neither of the two assumptions can be verified, and naturally you cannot quantify either. They are characteristics of experience in the form of assumptions. The one form of expression emphasizes the long-lasting consequences of a trauma, the other the necessary amount of strength that it used up at the time. This is not intended as an excuse, it may simply serve to illuminate the mechanisms of denial a little.

As for the reconstruction of the event as a whole, it is significant that he wrote that the handover of the money must take place "today." He was working, from now on, on the assumption that the abductors would use a fax machine, so that the letter would be received and acted upon the moment it was dispatched. And he also assumed that the abductors would work quickly. The letter is dated April 3 (Wednesday); he therefore assumed that the next handover should, indeed would, take place at the earliest on Wednesday night (he tried to apply pressure about this), more probably Thursday, at the latest Friday. There was some reason for this, since they had first told him that if all went according to plan, he could be home by Easter, and then, if it worked *this time,* that he could be home by Easter Monday. There was always a built-in period of at least forty-eight hours to wait after the money had been paid.

Meantime, he prepared himself for the fact that they might perhaps cut off one of his fingers. One finger—we usually have ten; which one would it be? He added up his experiences to date and concluded from these that they didn't want to mutilate him just for the sake of it. So it would be the little finger of his left hand, being the least used. Or if they gave him the choice, that would be his decision. He used the ample time available to him to say good-bye to it, because this would be the one he could most easily do without. I do not play any instrument and have my own system for touch-typing in which the left little finger is never used. He wondered if it would be easier to do without a toe (presumably all that was wanted was a bloody "Ecce") and decided that the problems following on the amputation of a toe would probably be greater. Skiing, for one. But primarily on the walk from wherever they would let him out of the car (if he survived at all) to some place of human habitation. You can see that the span of his feelings oscillated from death to alpine holidays, which should not seem so very remarkable. The most serious, brutal reality was constantly tangling itself with the unreal. Having a finger cut off—it was a reality straight out of some Mafia film that he had woken up in. So he and his finger took respective leave of each other. And this with a certain regret that he could have made better use of it up till now.

He was not so afraid of the pain. Many soldiers have amputated or shot off a finger in order to be declared unfit for the front. It was endurable. He was more afraid of the "how." That the kidnappers, in order to preempt any struggle and resistance, would come storming into the cellar at night, masked, seize hold of him and take a knife to . . . The additional shock of a repeat of his abduction, this time not with blows to his head but a mutilation, would be like some sort of progression, and he was afraid of that. It would be much less bad if he could retain a little control over this brutal operation, if it could be brought as close as possible to a medical procedure. He went so far as to wonder if he would look or not.

What preoccupied him was the possible timing of the mutilation. He calculated that the earliest it would happen would be Thursday and worked out the following: the finger would have to be sent by mail. If it were thrown into the mailbox on Thursday, it could not arrive on Friday—that was Good Friday. Is mail delivered on Easter Saturday? He didn't know. That is to say, there was a likelihood that if they cut off his finger on Thursday or Friday, it would not arrive in the mail until the Tuesday after Easter, which meant that the earliest next attempt at contact would be Tuesday evening, because the kidnappers would want to guarantee the effect of the amputated finger. So he might have to spend six days with his wound before the next time for a handover of the money could be set. Six days without adequate medical attention, with a real likelihood that the wound would become infected. So there was a risk of death from another source—gangrene. Were the kidnappers thinking this far ahead? He couldn't tell, so he wrote a letter laying out his arguments. If they intended to hack off his finger, would they please think about the problem of mail delivery, and if they were going to proceed, not to do so before Monday. In addition, he was requesting bandages, sufficient clean water, and painkillers. If they had considered the possibility of infection (perhaps they were equipped with medicines for all eventualities), he would like to call their attention to the fact that he was allergic to penicillin but could tolerate nonpenicillin antibiotics. He folded up the letter and wrote on both sides: "If you want to cut my finger off—read this first!!" He pushed the piece of paper into his sleeve so as to be able to pull it out immediately if things began to happen. At night he pushed it under the mattress, and whenever there was a knocking at the door he pulled it out in a flash and held it in his closed hand, ready to show. But nothing happened. The next hand-over went wrong, too, but they still left him physically unharmed. On Monday he tore up the letter and threw it in the wastebasket.

In fact, as previously indicated, there had been no attempt to transfer the money. Nonetheless, he was told that there had been yet another failure because of the presence of the police. The next letter from the kidnappers said the same thing, and like them, he wrote to Clausen and Arndt, the subsequent money carriers, about the failed attempts. Afterward he learned that the kidnappers had wanted to call during the night of Easter Friday but had not done so. Presumably they had already broken off the attempted contact because of actual or suspected wide-ranging police presence.

From Easter Sunday through Easter Monday, he had to write another letter. As always, he was allowed his choice of words. He was only told that it was up to him to make sure that things finally worked out this time:

April 7–8, 96

Dear Kathrin,

Dear Gerhard,

Please first discuss this letter between yourselves before you discuss it (if at all and if absolutely necessary) with anyone else. I am not under orders to write this letter—I cannot prove this, but it is the case.

Dear Kathrin—This evening I have been here for two weeks, and there have been nothing but failed attempts at contact and transfer of the money. For fourteen days I have been chained in a locked room (a detail I had spared you for the sake of your composure as well as my own—the 18,000 steps were three forward, three back) and just happy still to be alive. It is incredibly hard for me to think about you both, and when I look up the date in the Chronicle *every day at 5 p.m., my heart goes into spasm. I love you both—get me out of here soon, not sometime but in these next few days, I beg you!*

Dear Kathrin, dear Gerhard—every delay raises things to a higher power, without anything being accomplished by the time gained except the further draining of my mental reserves (and the further, perceptible angering of the people who brought me here). According to what I was told, the area of the first attempted payment was under police surveillance—and they noticed. During the telephone call on Saturday evening or night, there was a policeman listening in, as they could tell (thanks to having to repeat the names "Ingrid" and "Dührsen" three times, which should have caused you no difficulty, Gerhard)—which suggests to me that my kidnappers are behaving more professionally than the police. The result is it will be Tuesday before you even get this letter. Then the next identity check, the next appointment . . . I beg you, let this be the last time! If it goes on the way it's been going, it can still take weeks. I do not know whether this would worsen my situation—it is quite likely—but even its mere continuation would be unendurable. Every further delay raises things to a higher power, as I said, because the identity checks naturally have the same effect. It is up to you both—and only you—whether the next handover can still take place this week, *and whether it will be successful or not—that is, will proceed without police involvement. If it goes wrong again, who knows how long things will go on, and my will—excuse me, my strength—is at an end.*

Dear Gerhard—you are my lawyer. I hereby instruct you to organize the payment of the money without police involvement.

Dear Kathrin—please do the same. I can do nothing except write letters. Out there it is your decision which finally counts, and it is up to Gerhard to convince the police of this. I want to get out of here, I have to get out of here! Please, Kathrin—for Johann, for you, for me! Believe me, no further delay can produce the certainty that everyone would like to have in a situation like this— quite the contrary! Kathrin, give Johann a hug for me (I miss you both every minute).

Your Jan Philipp

If my memory is correct, the letter gives a pretty accurate picture of his view of the situation. He believed the kidnappers (whom, it is psychologically significant to note, he called "my kidnappers" this once, something he otherwise avoided, even in his diary), at least in general, since their assertion that they knew the police were back in the picture was the only explanation for the delays which seemed plausible to him. He was indeed aware that the only source for his conclusions was the information given him by his abductors, which meant that his thinking was conditioned by their view of things, but they themselves could have no possible interest in delays. Nor, naturally, could his wife, but the police certainly could. What the Englishman said to him made sense: "The police want to catch us. And we make mistakes. Small mistakes, but everyone makes mistakes, and the more mistakes we make, the more information the police will get about us. They want to make us angry and nervous. The police don't care about you. Policemen are like gangsters—both are hunters. And we won't give up."

Without taking this particular piece of gangster psychology, which says a great deal about the Englishman's character, and incorporating it into his own thinking, he imagined police advisers telling his wife she would only see him again alive if they were successful in finding both the kidnappers and their hiding place. And naturally he hoped this might succeed. He imagined it: sudden noise, quick footsteps, shots— what else? Perhaps the criminals would open the door and shoot him out of revenge. He would have to get away from the mattress, get under the table, not because it would be safe there, because there wasn't anyplace in the cellar that was safe, but at least out of the direct line of fire that ran from the door to the mattress.

He hoped for such a development but didn't believe it would happen. He didn't believe in mistakes that could lead the police to the cellar. He judged the abductors to be too professional to make major mistakes, and indeed he ruled these out when they admitted that of course they made mistakes, small ones that is, and wanted to avoid making *lots* of small ones. He also developed the firm opinion that the Englishman himself could be a former policeman who had, so to speak, switched sides.

Then something happened that alarmed him: on the telephone, Schwenn had been asked one of the identifying questions that he had had to make up for the kidnappers, namely the one about the disability of the teacher Dührsen whom both of them had known. Not a question that Schwenn should have had to think about twice. Now, according to the Englishman, whoever it was on the telephone had had to repeat the question several times before being able to give the answer. So it had not been Schwenn on the other end of the telephone but presumably a policeman, and he had had to ask and to repeat the question loudly, until Schwenn whispered the answer. The fact that the telephone was being monitored didn't bother him, nor that it was someone from the police who answered it; what struck him was their amateurishness. Had it not even occurred to them to install a speakerphone or one with a series of extensions? If this was the case, then he was no longer surprised that the handovers had been rendered impossible by all-too-obvious police activity. Now what had been a baffling situation began to become a little clearer. He must argue against the idea that police control was essential to saving his life, and give his wife courage to overrule police advice. He was in no way convinced that he really would be released after the money was paid, but he wanted to precipitate matters toward a conclusion. Anything rather than more weeks to be spent in this cellar (and then perhaps to be murdered out of sheer frustration). This transformation from being trapped and ignorant into having a problem to solve (however approximate to reality that problem might be) helped him. The unfortunate "I can't go on" does appear again, but this time it is more contained because of the way he sets it down: "My will—excuse me, my strength—is at an end."

My readers should know that I am not a querulous man; this really goes to the heart of his psyche. He wanted them to make the speedy termination of his imprisonment part of their risk calculations, and to strike any thoughts of "just another few days and maybe we'll find out where they've got him hidden." (What he didn't know was that his abductors were using voice-distortion equipment on the telephone, and that Schwenn, who had indeed been on the telephone personally, could hardly understand the questions, which explained all the repetitions.) He also knew nothing about various pieces of amateurism by the kidnappers which I only learned about later. The exact role played by the police in the various attempted money transfers—particularly the next one in Luxembourg—is something I do not know to this day; all I do know is that his notion that his wife and his lawyer could have discussed the letter without the knowledge of the police was naïve. The letters were being intercepted at the post office and dealt with by detectives before being forwarded by courier hours later.

In the bottom right-hand corner of the letter he put a little notice: "Separate letter for Johann herewith" (so that the kidnappers would also pass this on, or, if not, so that he would at least know something was missing).

Dear Johann,

I hope I will soon be back with you both—I wish with all my heart that I could hug you and Kathrin again, and I long for our lovely, boring, normal routine!

For the more distant future, I've been thinking: After you graduate from school, would it be nice to go around the world together? Here's the route I'm proposing (you can check on your atlas):

Hamburg—Warsaw—Cracow—Prague— Budapest—Vienna—Florence—Rome—Naples— Athens—Delphi—Olympia—Aegean Islands (pause)— Istanbul—Ankara—Baghdad—Riyadh—Jerusalem/ Tel Aviv—Cairo—Addis Ababa—Nairobi—Harare— Madagascar—Seychelles (pause)—Ceylon—Bombay— Calcutta—Delhi—Nepal—Tashkent—Mongolia— Northern China—Japan—Taiwan—Southern China—

*Vietnam—Thailand—Singapore—New Guinea—
Australia (Darwin→ Perth→ Tasmania)—New
Zealand (pause)—Alaska—Vancouver—Quebec—New
York—Niagara Falls—St. Louis—Salt Lake City—San
Francisco—Mexico—Guatemala—Caribbean
(pause)—Peru—Brazil—Argentina—Tierra del
Fuego—Antarctica—Tristan da Cunha—South
Africa—Congo—Morocco—Spain—Paris—London—
Edinburgh—Faroes—Norway—Finland—Moscow—
St. Petersburg—Stockholm—Copenhagen—Hamburg.*

*That way we would see something of the world. You
can see I have the time to work all this out. Until soon, I
hug you.*

Your Father F.

After the letter had been picked up, it occurred to
him that the itinerary, which he had worked out in one
of his many idle hours, would become a subject for
various police or computer brains, and he could only
hope they would soon realize that there was nothing
behind it but the dream of a man chained in a cellar to
go on a round-the-world journey with his son, whom
he didn't know if he would ever see again. Later I discovered that the police had thought at first that he'd
gone mad, then, when corrected by his wife, really did
begin to rack their brains over some secret message—
and the omission of the German capital, Berlin, led to
questions about whether one of the extortion calls had
been made from Berlin.

He had no idea that the kidnappers meantime had
made a demand for an airplane. It would have severely

shaken his view of their professionalism and shown him that at least some part of the self-assurance they had displayed since the evening of the abduction was pure hubris. On the other hand, the demand for a plane might have been nothing more than a diversionary tactic.

He waited again. Learned about the phone calls to the house and the two hotels, because the Englishman uttered the opinion that his wife had been replaced by a police psychologist, and wanted to confirm this with him. He was told she had shown no trace of anxiety, was "far away" from a nervous breakdown. She was very aggressive. She asked, "Are you the man who kidnapped my husband?!" A piece of the world slipped back into its right place. "That was no police psychologist. That was her." The Englishman seemed convinced. Admittedly, the lawyer Schwenn had been incredibly fussy again ("He's still following the instructions of the police and tries to prolong the phone calls"), but he believed the assurances that the police would keep out of it this time. Although the police had been in the neighborhood of the phone booth in Berlin from which he'd made the call—he had had to hang up. The Englishman then said that the handover was to take place abroad. Across the border with twenty million in the trunk of the car. "They have to inform the police. Otherwise it would be too risky," he said to the Englishman. He wanted to create some awareness of the problems a money courier would face, and make clear that until just a few miles from the handover point, the police would *have* to be there in everyone's interest.

The handover was supposed to take place on Saturday night. The Englishman wanted to be back on Monday—on Monday night he could be let go. The Englishman was going to set off now, Friday. Was there anything he still needed? He asked, as he had done once before, for aspirin—he had a continuous headache. And nose drops—he could feel a bad cold coming on. He got what he asked for, plus flu tablets which he could use as pain medication. The cold stayed away.

However, it wasn't yet Monday but Sunday afternoon when he heard a door being thrown open upstairs and footsteps coming down the stairs. The police had been there again. And Schwenn had gotten together with the police in order to trick them again. In the hotel where he was supposed to have waited for a phone call, there had been a policeman waiting instead. The man had been unable to answer an identifying question. "We asked for the name of his late mother's former maid, and he answered 'Ingrid.'" That had been the name of Schwenn's mother, and a question about it had already been used as identification in a previous question. Perhaps Schwenn had misunderstood the question and missed the word "maid"? "No. The call was in German, and the German word is much longer. But nevertheless, we went on." Then Schwenn took far longer than he should have to get from the hotel to the handover point, and soon the whole place had filled up with unmarked police vehicles. "I know the place very well and there are never cars at that time. There were police. I saw them and they saw me. I had to leave." And "I know them. They all look the same." The police were still underestimating them—they were prepared for any eventuality, they could see everything, they had night-vision equipment. "And if they try to catch us, we'll open fire on them. It's not good to kill a policeman. If you do, all the police in Europe will be after you, and I don't want to spend fifteen years in a room like this." Stop fussing, he said to himself; if they do catch you, the European Human Rights Commission would step in. I won't pretend he didn't regret this, just for a moment. "And if they kill us, no one will find you here." Could he have been mistaken? "No, there were police, I'm sure. Hundred percent, hundred percent." He had known a paranoiac once, one of whose favorite expressions was "hundred percent," which he used whenever he was talking about his imaginary pursuers and their absolute reality. He suddenly had the thought that the Englishman, for all his procedural intelligence, could be skirting the borders of paranoia and could start seeing ghosts in situations of stress. If that were to be the case, he said to himself, his chances were slim. He pushed the thought away, because no possible solution to his problem could come of it.

The Englishman asked him if it were possible that his wife didn't want to pay. "And the lawyer does what she wants." What was he supposed to say? He had to talk him out of this and yet could not begin to explain the emotional bases of their life together. He tried to make things objective. The interests of the trustees and the lawyer. Those of his wife: "Money doesn't mean so much to her. For us it's not so important to be very rich. Money is just an instrument to get things done." The Englishman's objection: people get accustomed to having money. "This is a nasty world, you know. People get killed for less than twenty million." "Well, you're telling me!" One of the more remarkable exchanges ever heard in this cellar.

A series of exchanges. The Englishman was furious. Not only because of the failure of the transfer of the money per se but because of what he seemed to view as Schwenn's betrayal. The same anger also shows in the letter to Clausen and Arndt. The Englishman really seemed to look on his criminal activity as business; he set parameters for it within which it was possible to distinguish between respectable and unrespectable behavior. These attitudes of the Englishman were bizarre, but he hoped he could find some way to turn them to good use—in case the next attempt also failed. But the Englishman was also nervous. "We're running out of ideas!" This was a disturbing admission.

So they had not been prepared for it to take so long, and had only worked out two or three scenarios. They didn't want to work with Schwenn anymore: "He's not reliable. We need some people from outside. Neutral parties." It was not the first time that he had the impression the kidnapping seemed to be a patchwork of pieces from other kidnappings—the photo from the Schleyer case, the threat about the finger from Italian cases, and now it was Pastor Albertz.* He was asked to think of possible go-betweens.

In retrospect, I have to say that despite the shock of hearing that yet another handover had gone wrong, that Sunday evening and the following Monday were the best days of his captivity. These two days provided the most to think about. The euphoria that sprang from the simple opportunity to use his mind, and in such a way that it would produce results, lasted until Tuesday, when his mood dissolved into two days of depression and fear which made him set down his last wishes in writing, and, in case of a de facto death sentence from thirst in the cellar, yet another farewell letter. But first, back to the question of names.

He was not sure what kind of "neutrals" the kidnappers had in mind. It was not clear to them, either, since they made no proposals of their own, despite his request that they give him some kind of example, other than "someone from the church perhaps." He was fixated on the Albertz example, which made him think of "church" and "politics." He did not belong to any church, and could not think of any pastor except for the one who had conducted the funeral for his mother two months earlier. So—politics. An ex-politician. Someone with a name. The first that came to mind was Klaus von Dohnanyi. He asked: "What do you think of someone like Klaus von Dohnanyi? He's the

---

*Pastor Albertz volunteered to accompany a group of released terrorists to the Middle East as a personal guarantor of their safety, in order to secure the release of a Berlin politician who had been kidnapped.

former lord-mayor of Hamburg. He knows me, I know him. He's now active in East Germany, and I do not know his address, but it should be easy to find out." The Englishman agreed: that sounded like a good idea. "Politicians want success." Yes, but.

During the night, he went over things again in his mind and came to the conclusion that he was about to set something suicidal in motion. Dohnanyi would surely be ready to offer his immediate help, of that he had no doubt, but first, it was more or less certain that Dohnanyi would do nothing against the advice of the police, and second, the arrival of a politician in such a situation would raise the numbers of police called in to be on hand just in case. Dohnanyi would have no possibility of deciding to act without police surveillance. So he dropped the idea of Dohnanyi.

What criteria must this person satisfy? He must be well known to the kidnappers, he thought. He must be credible to everyone involved. He should probably be reasonably well known or play some public role. This person could not be dependent on him. He must want to save him. He realized that there weren't that many people who fulfilled all of these conditions. He took a sheet of paper, wrote down names. Wrote. Discarded. Then there, without any deductive effort, was the name of Lars Clausen. The name stuck. Lars Clausen. If I reconstruct the idea, what I get is the following: Clausen was sufficiently public a figure, through his position as professor of sociology at Kiel and chairman of the German Sociology Society, to satisfy the kidnappers. He would probably carry some personal authority, although not so much official authority, with the police.

The latter was important, because Clausen had to get hold of the money somehow, and here I have to add something. Sitting in his cellar, he had no idea, I must repeat, of the situation into which he was sending his letters. He asked himself the classic question: Can a very good chess player who only knows white's moves reconstruct the whole match? He only knew white's every third move and was also probably being lied to. At some point the Englishman had said to him that they had left a live hand grenade on the letter at his front door. When had his wife noticed his absence and gone looking for him? Where had the letter and the hand grenade been lying? Could she have tripped over the grenade? Was she dead? The questions he had had to answer and the questions he had been reading in the announcements in the *Hamburg Morgenpost* could have been put by his son; they were all drawn from their private family language. The thought: And if all goes well, and I come home, then I hear "Your wife is dead. . . ." He put the thought aside. He managed to cover it with the taboo of the unthinkable. All that remained was: Then I have to survive for my son's sake. That made him hatch two plans in case of a further failure.

He had to find someone who could go to his house, the temporary occupants of which were likely to be complete strangers, introduce himself by letter and by personal authority, and collect 20 million. Clausen. He also thought that Clausen probably thought rather the same way that he did. Whatever might be going on over in Blankenese, he would like to be able to know that Clausen's voice, his way of thinking, were part of it. That was the most important thing, the actual reason for his decision. (Clausen's role thereafter was quite other. Clausen had no need to play the adviser. Yet the rightness of his decision in the cellar was something I learned later. His wife had asked Clausen to listen to the advice of one of the two private security men who were helping to prepare the last handover of the money, and Clausen answered that he would be glad to, but that he would be the one to decide what to do.) But Jesus!—did Clausen have a driver's license? He didn't know.

The Englishman had kept bringing the church into the discussion—for whatever reason. Perhaps it satisfied his movie-script mentality, perhaps also some peculiar concept of honor (you will not be deceived by a pastor?). The problem was as already stated. He didn't know anyone. Should he ask the bishop of Hamburg to delegate a pastor? That seemed absurd somehow, would also take days and would surely not remain secret. Then he realized that he did indeed know a pastor, it was just that he knew him in a non-religious context. Christian Arndt, of the congregation of St. Pauli. They had both been members of the mediation team in the fight over the Hamburg Harbor Road in 1987. So he wrote down this name, too, and mentioned that Christian Arndt's well-known critical attitude toward the government as well as the police could be both a disadvantage and, possibly, an advantage. Arndt would certainly have no instinctive personal impulse to cooperate with the police, but on the other hand could attract an awful lot of attention to himself.

There were other names on the list, but I will not mention them here. I neither want to make anyone's spine crawl in retrospect nor offend anyone for being left off. Anyhow, the Englishman agreed to approach both Clausen and Arndt and to ask them both to carry out the handover. He telephoned them and reported back that same evening. Clausen, according to the Englishman, had been utterly flabbergasted and unwilling to believe it. He would of course make himself available if a letter came from Mr. Reemtsma proving that this was not some "grisly joke." (Later Lars Clausen told me that he'd already very recently heard the news. He played his part perfectly.) Arndt, too, was instantly ready. He merely pointed out that there might be a tap on his telephone. The Englishman was delighted: finally a pro—and one disliked by the police. Now the letters. Oh—and by the way, the ransom was now thirty million. This increase was threatened before Luxembourg and must now be implemented. They had not carried out the threat to cut off his finger.

Did they imagine that he simply printed money at home? He knew that it wouldn't be hard to put together twenty million. He had heard once that the police could rapidly assemble such sums in kidnapping cases and loaned them to the families of the kidnap victims. But another ten on top?

At the very least it would take time. He said this to the Englishman. No problem, they needed time, too, to work out a new handover scenario. He wrote in his diary: "I must prepare myself for another two weeks (if all goes well!)." He wasn't wrong. "You could have been free after one week. You're still here and it's costing you ten million more. Thank your stupid lawyer."

To Lars Clausen
Dear Mr. Clausen,
Yes, it's true: I was seized in front of my house three weeks ago and since then I have been chained in a cellar somewhere in Germany. The ransom demand was for twenty million, but now, after three failed attempts to hand over the money, it has risen to thirty million. There was contact of every sort—by fax, by telephone, by letter, by newspaper announcement. Appointments were set— everything failed. I only know what happened from what I have been told, of course, by the people who are holding me here, but it all sounds quite plausible. The first time, the man selected by Kathrin, Gerhard Schwenn (from the law firm Senfft, Kersten, Schwenn), did not come (a picture of me which they had demanded had not arrived); the second time the place was under police surveillance, the kidnappers noticed this and left. Then there were problems on the phone, G.S. was replaced by a policeman and could only answer certain identification questions after they were repeated loudly several times (and followed by whispering). There were further telephone contacts, which did nothing to ease suspicion, but nonetheless a third attempt was organized in

Luxembourg—police there, too, and the kidnappers aborted the handover. I cannot judge whether they merely imagined police surveillance in either of these cases, but am inclined not to believe this. From the moment of the abduction itself it has been clear to me that I am not dealing with amateurs, nor with people who make mistakes out of sheer nervousness. I do not know how many there are, but there are several, with self-assurance to match: as far as they are concerned, they say, things can continue this way for quite some time, but on the other hand the room for maneuver is shrinking and patience has its limits. And that brings me to myself. Every delay has not only drawn the affair out longer but intensified it, since new security checks, etc., keep having to be made. Every day uses up some of my resources, I have a wife and son at home who do not know when, or if, they will see me again—I am trying to avoid such thoughts, as they would be hard to endure. Enough. On the side of the kidnappers there is no further trust in G.S.; I believe that for honorable but short-sighted reasons he is following the advice of the police (and they, as I need not tell a sociologist, will never say: Leave us out of this). Even Kathrin seems unable to impose her own decisions—or perhaps the police are acting without regard for her wishes?

In any case, there is no sense in beginning the fourth attempt in the old way. For this reason I have nominated you and Pastor Christian Arndt to conduct the negotiations with the abductors and to organize the delivery of the money. I know that this is an imposition on you, but *there are not many people who (a) are not dependent on me; (b) outsiders; and (c) friends of mine. I am deeply grateful that you already confirmed your willingness to do this on the telephone. I ask you please to ensure that the thirty million are handed over without involving the police. And as soon as can possibly be arranged. Twenty million are organized already, and I have written to Kathrin asking her to arrange for the other ten million to be put together.*

Dear Mr. Clausen, once more: forgive my asking, but I have no other course. If you are prepared to do this for me, I empower you and Pastor Arndt to deal on my behalf (and for my person) and to hand over the money.

Naturally you are asking yourself to what extent I am writing this letter out of my own free will. I am chained up and I am afraid. And I *do believe—and have reasons for doing so—that* payment of the money without police involvement *will mean the greatest safety for me. A phrase for identification purposes whose truth only you and I will know, no matter how many people handle this letter: Mr. Fohrbach's favorite author is Hackländer.*

Dear Mr. Clausen, *I hope we will see each other soon, so that I can thank you (I thank you already).*

Your
somewhat desperate* right now
Jan Philipp Reemtsma

Beneath this the address of Christian Arndt, which the kidnappers had found and jotted down for him, and a footnote referring back to the asterisk next to the word "desperate": "*It *must* work this time. I *cannot* wait any longer."

To Christian Arndt
15:4:1996
Dear Mr. Arndt,

You have been informed today of my kidnapping three weeks ago. I have spent the time since then somewhere in Germany, chained up. There have been various contacts with my wife and our lawyer (Gerhard Schwenn of the law firm Senfft, Kersten, Schwenn), three attempts to pay over the ransom—all of them failed. I have written in greater detail about this to Professor Clausen, whom I have asked for help, as I am asking you. You will certainly exchange letters. The kidnappers have lost all trust in the lawyer and I too believe that—for honorable but short-sighted reasons—he is following the advice of the police (and they will never counsel their own exclusion). I do not know whether my wife cannot impose her wishes, whether she shares the police view, or whether the police are acting without consultation. Perhaps they all under-estimate the professionalism of the kidnappers, who (as was very soon clear) are anything but amateurs. I don't know how many there are—several. After three botched handovers, they have raised the ransom from twenty million to thirty million.

Whichever one of the possible interpretations is correct, it is pointless to allow a fourth attempt to follow the third using the same cast. I have nominated you and Professor Lars Clausen to conduct negotiations with the kid-

nappers and organize the payment of the ransom. I know this is an imposition on you, but there are not many people who are both outsiders and connected to me by shared activities and not dependent on me. I am extremely grateful that you already gave your agreement on the telephone. If your agreement still holds *(and again, please forgive this request but I don't know any other course to take),* I empower you and Professor Clausen to act on my behalf and for my person and to pay the money.

Permit me to add a personal observation: each failed attempt has not just cost time, it has cost incremental time, since the security checks are becoming more and more detailed. Three weeks under these conditions (a family at home with no idea when or whether they will ever see me again) are immeasurably long, and I am using up much of my strength each day from a reserve that is in any case limited. (Enough of this!)

You are naturally asking yourself to what extent I am writing this letter of my own volition. I am chained up and I am in fear. And *I do believe—and have reason to do so—that the safest thing for me is* for the money to be paid over without police involvement. *For identification purposes, a fact that only you and I, of everyone who handles this letter, know to be true: the first name of one of the members of our mediation group in the Harbor Road business was Hans Joachim.*

Dear Mr. Arndt, *I hope we shall see each other soon, so that I can thank you (as I do already).*

Yours,
Jan Philipp Reemtsma

Lars Clausen's address and phone number followed.

To his wife (the Englishman rejected a first version of this letter because he considered it too cool and self-controlled):

15.4.1996

Dear Kathrin,

Tonight I could have been with you both. Yesterday I received the news: another failure, police everywhere. I don't know what to make of it. Believe me: the safest thing for me is for the money to be handed over without the police! Or is it possible that the police are acting behind your back? Of course, it could also be that the kidnappers have lost their nerve and are seeing ghosts— but they don't give that impression. These are not amateurs! I am trying to put myself in your place and am finding it very hard, because it makes me want to weep and if I do that, I've had it.

And if I think of Johann! But you must think of it as a brutal way of winding up a business deal, and it will work: money out, JP back. (It is so hard—not difficult but hard—to write to you, I am holding what's left of my little soul together by thinking distracting thoughts, but how long can that go on?)

To the facts, short and simple: They have raised the ransom from twenty to thirty million. Please get the extra ten million organized—*They do not trust Gerhard anymore. I also think that a new version of the old attempts will be unproductive. That's why I have* asked for two outside mediators and authorized them *to lead the negotiations and pay out the money: They are Lars Clausen and Christian Arndt. Both have already confirmed on the telephone that they are ready to help.*

It's the best way. People from outside can get some movement going in this. Everything has become completely knotted, and the prospect of having to spend weeks and weeks here is appalling! Oh, Kathrin, I don't want to wail and cry and make your heart even heavier than it is already. Give Johann a hug for me and hold each other tight! And let's hope it goes right this time. It has to work! I cannot go on waiting.

I love you both so much!

Your despairing

Jan Philipp

(I am enclosing something for Johann which doesn't sound so miserable.)

To Johann

Dear Johann,

I had so hoped to be able to be back with you again soon (and was feeling quite superstitious when I saw what happened today, April 15, in 1960—well, there you are, that's why you shouldn't be superstitious!). We must just keep holding on for a bit. It will come out all right.

Do you know how much I love you?

I bet you have an idea. Till soon, I'm sure.

Your father, F.

Superstitious: The *Chronicle* for this date listed the release of a child who had been kidnapped from the Peugeot family.

After he had handed over the letters, he saw an announcement in the *Morgenpost* asking for another proof that he was still alive. He asked if he could add the relevant answer to the letter. He was refused. First, these were just routine police announcements (this, as I later learned, was quite true), and besides, there would be no further contact with his wife, even his letter to her would be enclosed in the letter to Lars Clausen. Sharp, still very angry: "We won't have any further contact with your family! On principle!"

That was Tuesday, April 16. On Friday they would speak to Clausen and Arndt together. The Englishman was calm again. He had spoken with Arndt, who had been quick, clear, and precise. "He didn't play around and ask silly questions like your lawyer." Did he know a Michael Herrmann, and was he reliable? He was apparently supposed to replace Clausen as the second money carrier. "Perhaps Clausen can't drive or is too old." Yes, Michael Herrmann was reliable. No, he wasn't worried that he might take the money and run.

The odd thing is that Arndt had indeed said that Herrmann had taken over contact with the family, but not that Herrmann should be the second money carrier. In any case, as already mentioned, the police promptly accepted the idea that Herrmann was to hand over the money. This is yet another proof in support of the interpretation that the kidnappers had, by who knows what means, received information from Hamburg. Another followed soon afterward. "Maybe your wife has thrown the police out of the house," the Englishman said at some point, and the phrase "thrown them out of the house" haunted its way through the ranks of the police (and cropped up again in the press). The routes by which such details reach the perpetrators can naturally be many and various. The possibility that the source of the information was somewhere inside the police force is no more than a theory, but just as much a matter for routine consideration as the police having to weigh the possibility that he had faked his own kidnapping. Another possibility is the press. Speculation about the number of the perpetrators appeared in the very first press reports, and may have achieved wider currency. After news of the kidnapping spread, the press besieged our house, and Michael Herrmann had been seen. The idea that he could be the new money carrier may just have been general surmise. And finally, the press saw that the police were leaving our house. The phrase "his wife has thrown the police out" could just be the thriller version of the observed fact that the police did leave the house. I assume that the police at some point did some intentionally visible surveillance of Arndt and Herrmann—again, this will not have escaped the journalists, who must have started doing research as soon as Herrmann appeared. Because the press was holding to its promise of silence, there was no published scoop or exclusive report, and everything became instant Hamburg gossip instead. All the kidnappers may have needed was a listening post in the city, someone who frequented the relevant bars—i.e., the ones where the police reporters and their hangers-on spent the evenings. However that may be, when ESPO started running things behind the scenes, the information was deliberately put about that the police were being shut out from now on, and the behavior of the kidnappers changed. Whereas before they had been laying great emphasis on the look of the bags in which the money was to be handed over, to impede the functioning of possible transmitting devices, etc., this had become irrelevant to them by the last handover.

He spoke once about their raising of the ransom: what did they imagine his financial circumstances to be? Oh, he had inherited three hundred million (they were badly informed) "and you should have tripled the amount." They were overestimating him. Did he pay taxes? Yes. Had he invested a great deal in real estate? No. Well then, he must have at least doubled his money. They were forgetting the large sums he had to pay out each year for the institute and other organizations for the public benefit. The Englishman said this didn't count. "If your trustees didn't double your money, they're ripping you off. I would have tripled it. The eighties were a gold rush." "Do you want to make me an offer?"

In the blink of an eye he was visibly becoming an idiot to the kidnapper. His wife didn't seem to want him back, his lawyer was leaving him in the lurch, his trust was being badly run, and he had allowed himself to be captured like a songbird. It was rather distressing, but somehow not the main problem. More interesting was what the Englishman revealed in this brief exchange. The unknown man whom the press styled "Superbrain," in contrast to his accomplices, whom they dubbed "the two stooges," presented himself in this mixture of play-acted professionalism and sheer showing off as some kind of financial criminal mastermind out of a movie. He wanted to "pull off the big one," had taken care of most of it, thought most things out, just not (like a typical idiot) what he should do if his plans didn't work out exactly. Which is why, out of sheer amateurism, it took almost two weeks from the failed handover in Luxembourg to the planned date of the next. Also, the Englishman's thinking was one-dimensional, and, as I later discovered, took no account of the consequences of his and his accomplices' actions either for himself or for them. The kidnappers were sloppy. They couldn't figure out how to send faxes without the sender's number showing. They were no good at using the voice-distortion equipment they got for their subsequent phone calls. Most of all, they couldn't give clear directions to the people bringing the money: they kept confusing highway interchanges with road junctions, couldn't read maps properly, etc. In retrospect, I'm happy that he had no idea of all this in the cellar, even if this ignorance, as I've said, forced him sometimes to adopt the kidnappers' point of view.

When he spoke to the Englishman about the raising of the ransom, the latter said it wasn't a matter of the extra ten million, it was the principle of the thing: "We have to punish them." A remarkably inflationary mentality. "Maybe we can't transport the ten million, I don't know, I don't want to cut a lot of paper into little pieces to find out." Inflation: the unplanned money—a substitute for a finger and worth somewhat more than just one finger—metamorphosed into a pile of paper. But the pile of paper must already have been part of their plans, in the form of the question of how large a container must be to hold twenty million in denominations of one thousand, how heavy it would be, and so on. For him in the cellar, the money was *ransom* money, nothing more. Nevertheless, when the sum went up, he thought about the consequences: all the things that could have been done with this money, which now, before it could be partly gambled away and squandered by the criminals on riotous living, and partly used to set up further crimes, would have to pass through the hands of money launderers. What, he asked the Englishman, would he do with the money he couldn't carry? Naturally he'd be glad to have it back, but above all he was asking him not just to throw it away in the woods. He saw this as a risk, given the whatever-we-can't-use-is-mere-paper mentality of the kidnappers, and conjured up the headlines that would run if he were to be released: "Reemtsma Family Pays 10 Million Too Much. Blackmailers Simply Throw Money Away!" He could foresee all the letters from people who—not unjustifiably—would be of the opinion that part of the surplus money would have been better off with them than flying around in the woods. The concept of a bundle of cash carries with it very different ideas of how it should be properly spent than the information that twenty million has been spent to test-market some trademarked article or that a bridge which collapsed right before its dedication had cost two hundred million to build.

He also realized that this kidnapping would increase the risks in his life (the nature of many of the letters I received later only proved this), and with headlines like that, only more so. "No one has been kidnapped twice" was the Englishman's retort, revealing his peculiar attachment to precedents. He had, it seemed, done a great deal of reading on the subject and considered himself an expert who knew what could and couldn't happen.

He wanted to find out a little about the Englishman, and in the second half of his time in the cellar he tried repeatedly to draw him into conversation—cautiously, for he did not wish to find himself in receipt of any information that might be too revealing. He spoke to him about the level of expense and logistics that such a kidnapping must involve, and was told: to make each phone call they drove several hundred miles, to prepare for each handover they had to steal several cars, preparations for the whole thing had cost two hundred thousand marks.* Had he misheard? Two hundred thousand marks sounded to him like far too much money. On the other hand, what did he know about the number of accomplices receiving a prepaid lump sum? How much was the fee for a professional hit man like the one who had overpowered him and was apparently "long gone"? As I learned later, the renting of the house with the cellar cost about twenty thousand marks. Had he ever wanted to use his talents in another profession? "I didn't inherit three hundred

*About $115,000.

million, and you don't know what it's like to live on three or five thousand marks a month." "Don't under-estimate my imagination. But I meant jobs with much higher salaries." "Well, you'll be fifty or so before you earn real big money, and then your life is over. And don't forget: now I won't have to work for years!" Just years, not the rest of his life? Thirty million should surely be enough for lifelong luxury, if you're reason-ably careful and don't start setting up costly founda-tions (this sarcasm naturally remained unspoken): "You will enjoy the money?" "Of course!" "Well, it's a lot of money for one person. Of course, I don't know whether you work on your own or if you're part of a larger organization." That was far too risky a remark, and the Englishman didn't reply.

Another time: "Why did you choose me? I know it was easy to capture me—but before you found that out, what was the reason for focusing on me?" "We have a list. And we thought it should be easy with you. You don't need the money to maintain your lifestyle. You didn't earn your money, you inherited it, and someone who didn't work for his money will give it away more easily." "And how did I get onto that list?" "Some of the interviews you gave last year." (There hadn't been so many, only one with national distribu-tion, a conversation with *Spiegel*.) "But it was not that easy. It took us six weeks to find out where you live. And then you were on holiday for two weeks." So they had been watching him for weeks, and two weeks of school vacation on the ski slopes had made a mess of their timetable.

And finally: "Do you ever think about the price people have to pay for what you're doing? I'm not talking about the money." "You mean the moral question involved?" "Yes." "Well, you think about that beforehand. You don't start a thing like this and suddenly say to yourself: Oh my God, what am I doing? As long as you don't hurt people or do worse things to them." So that was how it was supposed to go: everything short of murder and mutilation was "just business," and if that wasn't how it went, people's deaths were certainly one of the eventualities built into his plans, as the Englishman himself stated repeatedly, and also put in letters or made other people put in letters. "We will certainly kill Mr. R." "We will open fire without warning." "No one will find you here." But he kept trying to paint a picture of himself, and of the situation he had created, in which he was the impartial businessman and rejected responsibility for everything that could wipe out the image of a transaction that was admittedly illegal but nonetheless defined by purely financial calculation.

This infantile trait was one of the most unsettling in the portrait of the Englishman which he had to construct out of the few sentences he heard. His beating was his own fault, because he had defended himself ("You must have been drinking, otherwise you wouldn't have fought"); as was the fact that the sum of money had had to be increased ("Thank your stupid lawyer"). So was his time in the cellar, quantitatively speaking ("It's been too long, but it would have lasted only five days or a week at the most if your family hadn't trusted the police") as well as qualitatively ("I wonder what you do all the time—I would sleep all day long").

In the final analysis, the Englishman seemed to believe that he had earned the extra ten million as a bonus, because when the Oetker kidnapping case came up twice in conversation—once as a kind of reproach, which continued the theme of "the moral question involved" ("You keep me here for days and weeks, my wife, my thirteen-year-old son don't know if they'll ever see me alive again"); the second time a kind of joke ("Thirty million—do you want to break the record of twenty-one million?")—both times the answer ran something like "Don't forget, they kept Oetker in a chest for forty-eight hours and gave him electric shocks." No, he never forgot that in the cellar, because he never forgot *what else* could have been done to him. That the Englishman wanted to be given credit for everything he did *not* do during the thirty-three days is a sign of significant moral degeneracy. An attitude that coexisted with a remarkable clear-sightedness about the significance and consequences of his act.

The Englishman enlarged on his remark that no one had ever been kidnapped twice, with the prognosis: "There will be other follow-up kidnappings, of course." The four kidnappings that would follow in the next six months—two of them ending in the death of the hostage—were also part of the built-in calculation of the consequences of this crime, as the Englishman cheerfully told him in the cellar.

He did not look forward to the next attempt at the transfer of the ransom with much confidence. The idea that the chain of failures would hold was dominant in his mind. It will not go well, he told himself. I will never get out of this cellar. Perhaps Clausen and Arndt will not be able to get at the money. It took the idea that something terrible could have happened with the hand grenade out there in Hamburg, that his wife might perhaps be dead and that all the failures to pay over the money could have sprung from that, to force him to think that he *could* not die, that he *must* get out of here, and that if the next attempt were to fail, then he could no longer leave it to the kidnappers to think up a new scenario, he would have to work something out himself.

But nothing came to his mind. If it goes wrong again, there's only one person who can get the money to the kidnappers, and that's me, he thought. But that is the absolutely most insane idea that anyone could try to put into the kidnappers' heads: to let your hostage go free and trust him to come back of his own free will with the money. So—it couldn't be "of his own free will." Or could it be possible that they would just give up? Just let him go free, because they didn't want to commit a murder that would bring them no money in any case? What could cause them to break their word and kill him anyway once they had the money could just as easily argue for them avoiding murder. They didn't have to keep their word once they had given it, because they didn't have to worry about anyone believing them twice. People usually only kidnap someone once; they are not in a marketplace where they can forfeit their credibility.

He began to write a letter to his abductors asking for mercy. He described his current situation, wrote that he wasn't well, that he was beginning to have serious worries about his health if his imprisonment in the cellar should go on for a great deal longer, that they would gain nothing from his death: "Be merciful and let me go." After this preparation he began to formulate his insane proposal. Then he suddenly realized that he still had another chance. This thought made him almost euphoric—until he was equally suddenly overcome by anxiety that he might no longer be thinking straight. Was it really a good idea, or was he letting his imagination run away with him? The plan was as follows, and began with the problem that anyone who was going to act as mediator first had to get at the money, which was to say, had to make contact with Blankenese and so would probably become known to the police. So he needed a money carrier who could come up with thirty million marks himself, and quickly at that. He thought of the *Spiegel*. Exactly a year before, he had done a major interview with *Spiegel* that was judged to have been a great success, and since then he had had good relations with the editorial board, who had, as already mentioned, invited him to do an editorial critique. *Spiegel* could get thirty million from the bank on short notice without further ado; i.e., the magazine could act without the police being any the wiser. And *Spiegel* would *want* to act without police knowledge. He would only have to describe the situation, guarantee in writing that the publisher would be reimbursed, whatever happened, and grant the magazine exclusive rights to his story. It would be a way to demonstrate risk-free journalistic heroism and achieve what had eluded the police, namely, saving the life of someone automatically made famous by the kidnapping, not an author, admittedly, but a profiled contributor and critic for the magazine. Not to mention a good chance of selling copies.

He worked through this proposal and then turned back to the first (which would also be the last, if it came down to having to make it). He tried first to arouse sympathy, to use it to make a space in the Englishman's head (since he was the only one he in some way knew) for some thought such as "Why should we actually kill the guy?" Then he gave the letter a new direction. There was another possibility, and one they should please not laugh out of court, although at first reading it must seem absurd. They could send him to get the money himself. Admittedly, why, once free, should he come back? He could only say, just because he had given his word. (Was the Englishman, who had been so furious at what he perceived to be Schwenn's double-dealing, perhaps susceptible to this idea of temporary freedom on someone's word of honor?) But of course it wouldn't be sufficient, and so all he could say was that he presumed that any breach of his word would not be forgiven—"and I don't want to live like Salman Rushdie for the rest of my life." It occurred to him that he was perhaps putting quite unpleasant ideas of future ways of getting money into the man's head, but at that point—I have to confess—he didn't care.

The idea was mad, and moreover it bordered on the morally dubious. Nor was it the only morally dubious matter he had to deal with in this cellar. He had not given Schwenn the task of being a money carrier, but he had nominated his bookkeeper, even though this was at the urging of the kidnappers, and this went right against a fundamental rule that he had set for himself. The naming of Christian Arndt and Lars Clausen gave him a bad conscience, too. For just as no one has the right to ask people who are employed by him to undertake such a job which is not without risk, so no one who is closely linked by friendship to someone and is asked by this person to save his life can refuse this request as an unreasonable demand. Under close scrutiny, his own actions in the cellar amounted to moral terrorism. Neither Arndt nor Clausen *could* refuse his request without very compelling reasons, such as illness. He had fallen prey to blackmailers and was now using moral blackmail himself. I am glad that he realized this while he was still in the cellar, and that he managed to allude to it in his letters.

He was faced with his next moral problem as he put his "last proposal" on paper. He had already fantasized scenarios for the handover in which money was directly exchanged for a human being—very "scene-of-the-crime," very moonlit-meadow, bags of money, bound victim, kidnappers' helicopter as silhouette and sound track (ominous thrashing of rotor blades). No, seriously, it might come to something like that and then to a substitution—the offer of another hostage in exchange—to secure their retreat. Was he allowed to accept this? He decided: no. And devoutly hoped that he would be able to manage if things went wrong. I do not know the answer to this. I can only repeat that he himself was opposed to any suggestion in the previously mentioned "last proposal" that there be an exchange hostage to give the kidnappers security. He really did wonder if he should quote Schiller's "Surety."*

He didn't do so, didn't make the suggestion at all, because remembering this ballad made him realize that while he could take responsibility for his good intentions, he could not take responsibility for the chaos of contingencies that would follow.

He did not give the Englishman the proposals as laid out, but told him that in case there was yet another failure in the ransom transfer, he still had some ideas, in the hope that perhaps this would restrain the criminals from an immediate impulse to murder him, and at least gain a little time.

They needed until the following Wednesday to work out a new scenario. If all went well, then he, the Englishman, would be back on Friday—and if not, earlier. He could be free by Friday night. He would be let out of the car in a wood, where he would have a few miles to walk and then find somewhere to make a telephone call. "We'll give you a telephone card."

Wednesday. Another telephone call had taken

*The famous poem about Damon and Pythias.

place. A typewritten note was passed to him: Arndt had asked a question to establish whether he was still alive or not: "Where does Caraway the cat come from?" One-two-three-four-five-six. Is this what it's like when your heart stops? He didn't know the answer. He didn't remember anymore where the hell the cat had come from. Couldn't they ask something else? Kathrin's brother had originally brought the cat with him from somewhere in Schleswig-Holstein. But from *where*? Malente? It was something to do with Malente, but what? What happens now, if I don't know anymore? Then suddenly there was the name: Trittau. His wife had given the cat—a particularly enchanting calico creature—the ironic title "Miss Trittau." Miss Trittau. Trittau. He could prove he was still alive because he knew the name Trittau. He wrote it down. And in a fit of panic (had the Englishman understood the question properly?), he added a few more biographical details about the cat. To have in reserve. Just in case someone wanted to know. And in case Trittau still wasn't the right answer.

If everything went according to plan, he would get something in writing on Thursday morning. During Wednesday night, he was only to knock on the door in an emergency, "in case of fire or something." The person who would be guarding him would not come downstairs. He asked if the "guy" (his word) would bring him breakfast as usual or whether he should wait for him to bring word at noon. He didn't care about breakfast: he wanted to know how many hours there would be before he would no longer be able to talk himself out of panic. No, "the person upstairs—she won't come down." So, a woman. A woman who didn't want to come downstairs. Was she one of the gang, or did they have so few people that they had to draft one of their girlfriends? ("Well, okay, just for one night, but I am NOT going DOWN there!"—or whatever?) So they didn't just intend to leave him there in the cellar and disappear, or the Englishman would not have expressed himself with such unintentional precision ("person" and "she"), he would just have said: Don't knock on the door, we're there, but we won't come—so that he wouldn't knock, notice that he was alone, and start preparing to break out. The news that there was a woman up there above him who didn't feel safe coming down made him feel dangerous for a moment, and his self-esteem rose. I can add that the sheer silliness of this reaction was not lost on him in the cellar.

Suddenly he was seized with anxiety again, that the lightbulb in the ceiling would burn out and he would be left sitting in darkness. He was forbidden to call attention to himself by knocking except in more obvious emergencies. The Englishman (with a shrug over this piece of neurosis) gave him a replacement bulb and, with a certain evident irony, two batteries for the camping lanterns, said a friendly good-bye, and left him with the warning: If they didn't come back, the woman would not let him out. "She will go away and leave you here."

One of the nights without much sleep. 4 a.m. 5. 6. Then he fell asleep. Woke up again. 8. (No major excitements before noon, is what he had told himself.)

Half past eight, knock at the door. Usual routine—head down. "Yes. Come in." Door opening. Footsteps. It is *not* the Englishman. The plate is set down. Sounds of paper rustling? Footsteps. The door. Look up. The basin has gone, the water is being changed. Table: paper next to the plate. He cannot read it, where are his glasses? Got them. Two lines: PASTOR HAS PAID AS PER INSTRUCTIONS. TOMORROW NIGHT YOU WILL BE FREE.

It was cause for jubilation, but he felt none. It could still happen that they were going to kill him and just wanted to keep him quiet for as long as possible. But he was thankful. What to do with his feeling when you have no God at whose feet you can lay it? There were spiders in his cellar, which were thriving on the dry air. In all the days he must have killed at least twenty of them, since he didn't like spiders, particularly when he imagined them running around him at night. After he had read the news, he saw another spider making its spindly way right across the carpet. He thought of the story from Johann Peter Hebel's *The Family Friend* in which a sailor bends down in the middle of a sea battle to pull an insect out of his hair, thus avoiding the fatal cannonball. So he didn't kill the spider. Nor any others in the time that remained. If you asked me what I would describe as "blasphemy," I would say: killing a spider in this cellar.

He had another two long days to wait. At the end of the first, the Englishman took his watch away and in a good mood told him about the pickup of the ransom:

They had been able to manage all the money. "We had to sit on the container, but we managed to close it." But they had driven the rental car in which Arndt and Clausen had come into the ditch. He was audibly embarrassed. "It was dark, we couldn't switch the lights on." Not, as was assumed later, a deliberate act. The criminals were nervous; they were not fully in control of themselves. They had even apologized over the cellular phone (the Englishman always called it a "mobile phone"). In this last moment, their self-image as perfectionists had taken a dent.

At the end of the second day, fear returned. He heard sounds of things being cleared away upstairs. Noises like bookcases being disassembled and the shelves removed. Then a clinking, as if bottles were being thrown into a container. Then silence for many hours. Should he knock? What if they were just taking their garbage away, a long way away, and didn't come back, but the time wasn't yet up? When would it be time to decide to try to break out? The chances of this were somewhat better than they had been at the beginning of the thirty-three days, because he had succeeded in hiding away three glass bottles, and maybe the plaster was soft enough for him to scratch out the dowelling that was holding the chain. What would happen if they caught him at it? The old questions, always the same. He waited. The Englishman came. A plate of bread. Water to wash. And his chain was undone. They wouldn't do that if they were going to leave him in the cellar! Enormous relief. It could still be that they were going to shoot him in the woods, but they were not going to leave him to die of thirst in the cellar.

At some point the Englishman came back and told him to close his eyes and sit on the chair. His eyes were covered with a bandage again, this time very carefully. His shoes were put on his feet, but he didn't get his clothes back. Why? Surely clothes don't carry fingerprints. "You can't make mistakes in a job like this." Could he take his notes with him? Of course not. He asked for two things. First, to be allowed to take toilet paper with him (he didn't know how long he would be in the woods, and his stomach was in rebellion due to the tension). And second: "I wrote a farewell letter to my family, in case something should happen. I wanted to smuggle it out, but I don't want to risk anything. So please keep it." "Okay. I'll destroy it." "Please keep it and destroy it when you read in the newspapers that I'm safe. If something happens, please send it to my family. I've told you what I'm asking you to do. You don't have to tell me whether you will do it or not."

The letter began roughly thus:

Dear Kathrin, dear Johann, if you receive this letter, I will have been killed by my kidnappers. I hope that at least they will have the decency to allow you both to receive my last greeting.

Then a few words similar to those in his first farewell letter and some amendments to his will. His hope was that if the kidnappers killed him in the wood, they would leave the letter by his body. This made him wonder if his body would be found in time for the letter to be still legible.

And another thing: "If you run out of money some-time—it won't be soon, I think—and if you plan some-thing new, please don't kidnap anyone again. You shouldn't do this to people." "Oh well, but you had the deluxe version of it, don't forget." It shot through his head that the Englishman would enjoy saying that to the court, but it seemed advisable to stifle that provo-cation. "If you have a business card, I could recom-mend you to anyone who wants to get kidnapped." The Englishman probably understood the irony in this, but not the play on Sigmund Freud's remarks about his treatment by the Gestapo—just like most journalists, some of whom showed themselves immune to both the irony of this reply and the cynicism of the Eng-lishman when they took a reference to the "deluxe kidnapping" from a conversation he had with the *Süd-deutsche Zeitung* and quoted it out of context.

His hands were bound in front of him with adhesive bandage. They were not going to gag him, "but if you shout, we'll make you stop." Then he was led out of the cellar. I hope I never see it again, he thought, and then: I hope I do see it again soon. In the company of the police. Up the stairs. He noticed that the steps had no risers. Once up, he was made to turn around sev-eral times. Then out. A car, not the same one that had brought him. He had to climb in at the back again, but this time there was no tailgate. "Is this a trunk?"

"Something like that." He had always been afraid of being carried off somewhere in the trunk of a car. He thought of Schleyer, and Aldo Moro.

The space was tight, he felt as if he could hardly breathe. Then loud music—he wasn't supposed to be able to identify any of the sounds of the journey. A radio or a cassette—he couldn't tell. Hopefully they'll leave it on, he thought. But there were only two or three tracks, then it was switched off. "Slow!" he heard the Englishman say. A short time later they were on the highway. "It will take some time, but we'll drop you off not far from where you live." He was not completely shut off in the trunk, there was a removable storage cover. Once he tried to move his body, bumped against this, and something fell down. "What are you doing?" This said in a furious tone. "I was trying to change position and something fell down." "Stay as you are!" A little later they had him memorize the number of the cellular phone his wife had obtained to communicate with the kidnappers; the Englishman had forgotten to bring the slip of paper he had jotted it down on for him. So they really didn't intend to kill him. If only to keep him calm, he thought, they could spare themselves this circus.

It was a long trip on the highway. At one point they seemed to be on an interchange. Hopefully they haven't gone first in the opposite direction just to confuse me, he thought, and now they're driving the whole way back! Then he heard a sound under the wheels that is characteristic of a stretch of highway near Soltau in the northbound lane.

The fan was working. But he couldn't move without hitting something and that made his claustrophobia more and more intense. So he tried not to move at all, because moving made the constriction of the space so evident, just his head a little, and his bound hands a bit to the left and then a bit to the right. He recited ballads to himself, and in retrospect I have to say that he very much underestimated the length of the journey when he told the police that they had driven for about an hour. For twice through "The Cranes of Ibycus" and twice through "The Reward" takes a good half hour, and Schiller and Droste-Hülshoff only occupied a small portion of the journey.

Then they were leaving the highway. A short stretch, then an unpaved country road. "Lights." Car stops. Trunk opens. The thought again: Are they going to shoot me now? The tape binding his hands was cut (after a brief whispered exchange with the person who had driven the car, because the knife was not immediately available). A telephone card was put in his palm. The Englishman had forgotten to bring any coins; the driver had none, either. Then the Englishman took him by the hand and led him into the wood. He felt like Hansel. It was cool and damp. The wood smelled of spring. For four and a half weeks in the cellar, he had smelled nothing but his food, the disgusting aftershave of one of his silent guards (twice), and above all the chemical toilet. Now this overwhelming smell of damp earth, grass, new leaves. He almost said something, and just managed to restrain himself. He didn't want to share this feeling with the Englishman.

Then they stopped. Now he could loosen the bandages over his eyes but must not look around, must just walk straight ahead and not back under any circumstances! "Some miles on there's a railway bridge, and beyond it there's a village called Horst. There you will find a telephone or a house where you can call your family or the police, whatever you like." He tore at the blindfold, couldn't find the tail end, yanked it over his head with no regard for his hair. Pitch-black night, clouds, no moon. He took a few steps. Should he say something? "Good-bye"? Hardly. How do you say good-bye to a kidnapper? "Nice to have met you, I can't say." Laughter. "I understand."

He walked. Under normal circumstances he would have felt uneasy in a dark wood with a long unknown path in front of him to who knows where. He also immediately thought of a quite unpleasant passage complete with a lunatic murderer in Stephen King's *Gerald's Game,* but somehow these imaginary figures no longer had the power to frighten him. He simply went forward, step by step, mechanically, not too quickly, because the path was uneven and he could hardly see a thing. How long? Perhaps half an hour, perhaps more. To his left, a few miles away, the roar of the highway. The path led to a slightly wider road, and an occasional car passed. Keep walking. The road dipped downhill a little. Then he saw the bridge and, behind it, lights. It's a feeling we've almost lost today, he realized, the feeling of safety when you come to the end of a wood full of robbers and suddenly see the lights of a village. There are hardly ever times when you know that you have absolutely no idea what may happen in the next few minutes. I love civilization, he thought.

Then he was in the village. No telephone booth in any direction. A sign: station, three miles. No, not another three miles. One house still had lights on; he looked through the window into the living room where a man was watching tennis on television. For a moment he felt like E.T.: "Phone home!" He went up to the house, rang the bell. Took a couple of steps back from the door in case the man should think he was going to attack him. How did he look, anyhow? He hadn't seen his own face for four and a half weeks. The door opened: "Yes?" "Please forgive me for disturbing you so late, I wanted to ask if I might use your telephone." "Provided you're not calling long-distance to Australia?" "No—Hamburg. I would like to call my wife. I can also explain why I'm standing here at your door in the middle of the night in such a mess. It's such a wild cops-and-robbers story that you will hardly believe it. I was kidnapped and I've just been released." "What! Should I get my gun?" "No, don't worry. It's over now."

It's over and yet it's not over, not by a long shot, nor will it be over when the criminals are sitting behind bars. The cellar continues to be part of my life. Which is why I want to go back to it, because some details have just been sketched in and could not do justice to events because of the way they were being presented. Even if I have written in a very restrained way, the drama of what I am writing about forces its way out, which is not wrong, since it was part of things, and yet it wasn't that much a part of his days in the cellar. These, as I have said, were like continuously treading water in a barrel without being able to climb out. I can catalogue the order of his days, even when there was none. The days differentiated them-selves according to the feelings that predominated in them, and the feelings were mostly—even if not com-pletely—conditioned by the timetable of the kidnap-pers and the information it brought with it. Yet I can describe the outward form of the days, which acquires something soothing in the telling that was absolutely lacking in reality. I have to separate the two strands of information: what I am going to write here should be linked by the reader with what I will describe later under the inadequate heading of "fear."

At some point he woke up. It was dark, not a single crack of light. He didn't look at his watch, tried to go back to sleep. Went back to sleep, woke up again. Then there was a knocking. Not for the first time, but the other times had been in his imagination and had always jolted him awake. He called out, "Yes! Come in!" Depending on who it was, the door was opened either quickly or slowly. Then the light was switched on. Footsteps. A plate was set down on the table. The person left, taking the washbasin. Came back a few minutes later bringing the basin with fresh water.

Differences: the knocking was different, depending on who it was. The ways of turning the key in the lock. One of them always switched off the light as he left (in the diary, he was called "the Cretin"). At the end there was someone who never brought warm water, only ice-cold (not a problem, but a sign that this person was a late addition). Someone, probably the Englishman, seemed to like eating corn flakes, and brought some for breakfast. These had to be eaten while the water for washing was being fetched, so that they didn't turn to mush. Twice he smelled a distinctly nasty after-shave or cologne that the relevant person must have splashed onto his face. Unfortunately the same hands had been used to cut the bread for breakfast, making it inedible.

For a time, breakfast came at 8 a.m. Then at 9, 9:30, 10—when the Englishman was there, it was usually at this later time. Maybe the Englishman liked to sleep later, suggesting a top position in the hierarchy, or maybe he wanted to let *him* sleep late, or maybe he was less compulsive than the other(s), who stuck miserably to eight o'clock. If it came after 9:30, he was well awake, waiting almost always in the dark, to which he had begun to accustom himself as the days passed. He wanted each day to begin in a regular way, with something requiring some minimum activity, and not with a vacant waiting for an indefinable something. If it hadn't come by ten o'clock, the fear would start.

He got up, washed himself after first refilling the water in the two spare bottles. He always had two, three, or four plastic bottles with drinking water, about 3½ pints each. He had saved two empty ones and filled them with fresh water from the washbasin in order to have an extra six or seven pints. Of course, there was always the used washing water in the basin, but that was soapy. Then he poured water for cleaning his teeth into the plastic mug he had been given. Next, he washed himself, standing with one foot in the basin and the other (because the chain prevented him from removing the pants of the sweat suit entirely) beside it. Last, he cleaned his teeth.

Then he lay down to sleep again and slept, if he was lucky, until around noon, which was mostly possible if he hadn't gone to sleep until just before dawn. If he was even luckier, there would be a knock sometime in the morning and the Englishman would bring him newspapers, usually the *Süddeutsche* and the *Frankfurter Allgemeine* and the *Hamburger Morgenpost,* because of the announcements. If there was anything in there to clarify—telephone numbers, identification questions, descriptions of people selected as money carriers—a short conversation would ensue.

At noon he ate a little and started reading the papers. If there were no new newspapers, he read part of the old ones—he always saved one section for the next day or the day after that—or part of the *Chronicle*. Two and a half hours until 2:30. Then he lay down on the mattress again, read the *Chronicle* for half an hour, and tried to sleep from 3 to 4, which almost never worked, but he forced himself to stick to this rest period in the middle of the day.

If he slept during the day, he never switched the light off. He didn't want to disturb the rhythm of day and night. From 4 to 5 p.m. he read bits of the *Chronicle,* then, as he had promised in the letter to his son, the "on this day" entry (which lasted a quarter of an hour). He went on reading (or tried to write, and usually failed) until evening, i.e., until around 8 p.m., when the morning routine (knock, arrival of food, removal and change of water) was repeated. He ate something, washed, cleaned his teeth, dampened his towel and laid it over the cover of the radiator to make the air a little less dry, and "went to bed." There he read the *Chronicle* for an hour or two. (In four and a half weeks he read it word for word and found several printer's errors as well as errors of fact and wrong or contradictory dates: he would have been glad to pass on his copy to the publisher.)

Then followed whichever book he had chosen for this time and rationed out in evening installments.

When he saw that the *Chronicle* was coming to an end, he curtailed these readings and instead used the evenings to read de Beauvoir's *The Second Sex,* which luckily he had never got around to before. Then—interrupted by a few stories of Dostoevsky's—first Le Carré's *The Little Drummer Girl,* then Wolfe's *The Bonfire of the Vanities,* then Lessing's *Going Home,* and finally Nadolny's *The God of Impertinence.* After Nadolny he read the Tom Wolfe novel a second time. Kraus, Jaspers, and the essays on Sloterdijk were daytime reading. The evenings and nights respectively were for literature, which, or so he hoped, stood the most chance of relaxing him. The little volume of Kishon and the book on the Mossad got slotted in on the side. At the end of the thirty-three days, the Chatwin and the Cronin novel remained unread (he hoped this would not be taken as a criticism), being held as emergency rations. Dostoevsky's short stories were the last reserve of all. He knew them and, in contrast to the novels, had never liked them. Besides, he had decided that if things dragged on for weeks he would have to switch to learning things by heart, and his choice for this was "The Dream of a Foolish Man."

He read until around 2 a.m. at least, sometimes until 3:30. He hoped that by then he would be tired enough to go to sleep without his mind racing too much. It sometimes worked. And sometimes he didn't drop into a sort of doze until almost 6 a.m. He never slept without jerking awake several times because he thought there was a knocking at the door. Right until the end he could not distinguish the imaginary knocking from the real knocking, and so called out several times each night, "*Ja!* Yes! Come in!"

During the day, he tried to do some exercises, if only to maintain his circulation. The longer he was in the cellar, the more often he began to have heart pains. Sometimes it was as if a heavy ring were being tightened around his chest (just like the fairy tale of the frog king: "No, sire, it is not the wagon, it is a band round my heart that broke and lies there aching"), sometimes it was a painful stabbing sensation, sometimes it had an irregular beat. He had never had heart problems, but it was clear to him that the fear and tension during this period would seek some somatic release, and he assumed that it would be his heart. So he wanted to give it mechanical work to do, and on a fairly regular basis.

The first week, he marched up and down in the cellar. That is, as far as the chain would allow him. Then he tried to go in small circles, but the chain became twisted and soon got shorter, so that he had to stop and go round in the other direction to restore it to its normal length. In the final analysis, seven feet of chain was not enough for going around in circles, so he walked up and down.

His walking soon took on a certain manic quality. It was the only thing he could "do." It ate up time, it saved on reading, it kept his circulation going, and above all, it stilled his thoughts and feelings. Masochistically, but also perhaps wisely, every time he miscounted he went back to the nearest hundred and started again.

He learned how many steps there are in a day. Three thousand, he estimated, amounted to less than an hour; four thousand were a bit over. The first day he didn't go that far, three thousand, perhaps five thousand steps. The next day, eight thousand, then fifteen thousand, then eighteen thousand five hundred. The day after that, fifteen thousand again. That became his daily task. Three steps forward, sometimes two and a half, then back. After two and a half or three steps he swung his foot out and around like a chained elephant, and then back, and then up and down again. Mostly in three-thousand-step sequences. Sometimes, when he was having a harder time, he walked even more pro rata.

His socks were soon threadbare. He walked barefoot. Made a mental picture of the distance. X number of miles. Began to invent stupid records for himself. So that when he got out he'd be able to say "I walked ———— miles."

But it only went okay for a week. Then his foot began to hurt in the morning. He kept doing his daily set amount. The foot became more and more painful. It was the left foot, the ball of the foot and the big toe, where he had to make the turn because of the chain. The next morning he could no longer put any weight on it. He figured it out for himself: probably an inflamed tendon. Like someone who types too much and isn't used to it. It didn't worry him, it just prevented him from walking. He had to find some other form of physical activity. The number of push-ups he could do one after the other would be embarrassingly small, as he knew. So he positioned himself at a distance from the wall, leaned forward until he could brace himself against it, and did "wall-ups," as he called them. Forty every hour. Then touched his toes. He spared his left foot, kept it off the floor while doing his "wall-ups." After another week, carrying all his weight on one side while doing the wall-ups had made his right foot swell, and it hurt so much that he kept jerking awake as he was dropping off to sleep, because his foot was cramping. He took some of the paracetamol tablets, which were supposed to work not just for flu but for pains of this sort. He decided they helped.

The left foot was in bad shape, too. He couldn't walk, only hobble. If they set him free now, then he would be incapable—"you'll have some miles to walk"—of going far. He would look for a stick and would soon be having to crawl along. Admittedly, this was a minor worry, but a worry nonetheless, one that had further mental ramifications. He would take pain medication before his release and remember to take more with him. Then he would just clench his teeth and keep going as far as he could. No fooling around. Try not to have to spend the night in the woods.

Aside from all this, it was of course embarrassing. He spends weeks in a cellar and comes out with inflamed tendinitis in both feet! Is set free and cannot even walk a mile or two because his feet hurt too much! Pampered philologist and scribbler from Hamburg-Blankenese. He would quite like to garner a little sympathy for having been beaten, dragged away, and chained up, and now he had to worry about reappearing as a clown. He considered asking the Englishman to get two elastic bandages from the pharmacy. But that was embarrassing, too. There was no relationship between the possibility of survival and release and the complaint "My feet hurt!" He hoped he would get better before the Monday evening when his release was supposed to take place, always assuming the handover of the ransom in Luxembourg went smoothly. But on Sunday afternoon the Englishman came back, and he had to hear that the handover had failed. Things lasted almost another two weeks, and it was yet another two weeks after his release before he could walk without limping.

Food. Mostly it was bread and cold cuts. Black bread. Rye bread. With ham, or sausage, or cheese, marmalade, cottage cheese, tomatoes. Once there was a breaded veal cutlet from a takeout place, once half a chicken, twice oversalted ravioli, twice lentil soup, and twice noodle soup—both heated up from cans. Scrambled eggs, oversalted, twice. One of the guards obviously liked eggs for breakfast and wanted to do him a good turn. So on three separate days he got three eggs each. Soft, cold, no salt. He tried not to draw any conclusions from this about the intellectual capacities of the team as a whole. On the first day they gave him spaghetti with a tuna fish sauce that was so greasy they brought him a glass of wine to go with it. This was the one exception: otherwise there was water from plastic bottles, and later there was long-life milk, too. The Englishman once apologized for the food: "The food is not very good, I know, but we eat the same." He was actually vying for understanding using the hoary old argument used by senior officers on long campaigns: they shared the hardships with the foot soldiers. Answer: "The food is the least of it." But he used the Englishman's apology as an occasion to make a suggestion: "Some fruit would be nice." From then on he always got an apple or a banana. Someone liked strawberries (it was still early in the year) and always put on his table whatever was left over in the little basket. In addition to the fruit, he also got fruit juice in—and this was crucial—glass bottles. This was the first time he had something to hand that wasn't paper or plastic. Something that could support fantasies of a breakout.

So he really could not complain about the care he was given; it was certainly their intention to feed him properly. Only when the uneaten pieces of bread began to mount up did they give him less at mealtimes. He wasn't hungry. Ate almost nothing the first day, and not much after that. He also drank very little—on the one hand because he simply didn't feel he wanted it (he was neither failing, nor was his body ready to enjoy anything), and on the other, because he had a permanent fear of being left behind in the cellar and dying of thirst, and he wanted to save what he had. After a few days the result was that his kidneys began to hurt. From then on he was careful to drink water in regular and sufficient amounts.

Naturally, the course of a day in a cellar is made up of little things, too, but they are different from the ones that make up a day outside. For example, it's different when you're chained up. Turning around causes problems; the chain gets twisted, which makes it shorter or tighter. Once he asked for the chain to be shifted from his right foot to his left. This was a mistake. His radius of movement was reduced, most of all when he was using the camp toilet, because he had to do this with his back to the wall, and thus the door, out of fear that he would never know when one of the kidnappers would come in. Admittedly, the man would knock first, but apart from the Englishman, he had no idea what language any of them spoke, not even if a "Just a moment, please," called through the door in either English or German, would be understood. The danger was that someone would confuse a request for a moment's patience with his "*Ja!* Yes! Come in!" and would walk in. That would certainly have been an embarrassment. But more important was his feeling that the kidnappers sometimes came into the cellar without their masks, and to see any one of them without a mask—as the Englishman had made plain—could be fatal. So, the toilet must be used with his back to the door. And with his back to the door, his left foot was further away from the place next to his mattress where the chain was attached to the wall. Similarly, when he wanted to reach the radiator thermostat, it was easier if he was chained by the right foot. The next day he asked that the old arrangement be reinstated.

If you're chained up, you can't undress, either. When you wash, your pants always stay tangled around the foot with the chain. He was allowed to change the sweat suit twice, at which points the chain was removed. There was one evening when he was given a plate of ravioli that was so hot he burned himself and spilled tomato sauce on both halves of his sweat suit. What should he do? Knock? He didn't know if the Englishman was there or not, or if anyone else would be able to understand him, and thought that they would only unchain him if there were at least two of them. Besides which, he would have to do what he always did for this procedure, which was to lie facedown, which would achieve what he wanted to avoid at all costs: getting the mattress and bedclothes covered in tomato sauce. So he decided to wash the sweat suit himself, which was not a problem for the top half. When he'd finished, he hung it over the radiator. But he could only soak the pants as far as the chain on his foot would allow. Most of all, he couldn't hang them up to dry. So he spread them out on the floor and tried not to pull them under the covers during the night. Of course, they didn't dry, and so sometime during the early-morning hours he put them on again and tried to dry the clammy material under the covers.

The chain also served to tell him how tall the Englishman was. When he was given the vacuum cleaner, he used the socket opposite the wall to which the chain was attached. It wasn't easy to reach it; he had to stretch out at an angle and the chain hurt his feet. (He hadn't noticed that there was another socket under the table, because all he did was throw the old newspapers under there.) In the evening, the Englishman checked the chain and asked how he had reached the socket: "It's not easy. It hurts." Amazing, he had tried it himself and couldn't reach the socket—another inspection of the chain. The Englishman seemed to have assumed that they were both about the same height, but in fact the Englishman was somewhat smaller. So that was how the length of the chain had been calculated: he was not supposed to be able to reach the opposite wall. Since there was, as already mentioned, another socket quite close to him, this could only mean that they wanted to keep him away from the radiator, because you can make a noise on a radiator that will echo through the whole house (presumably this also explained the cover on the radiator).

Were there people in the house from time to time who weren't supposed to know that there was someone in the cellar? (I later learned that the lady who had rented them the house had a set of keys and access at all times.) In any case, he did not let on that he could adjust the room temperature himself: if that had been known, his chain would probably have been shortened.

It is unclear how much really did depend on trivia like this—in his imagination, an enormous amount, even his life. If they left him behind, would he have a chance to make his presence known by banging on the radiator? Probably not, but you couldn't *know* that. I have already mentioned that when he entered the house and went down the stairs, he kept his eyes closed for fear that if he moved too confidently, he would make them suspicious that he could see something; this is also why he was truly frightened when he saw a sticker from the "Continent" supermarket on the first fruit-juice bottle. He immediately scratched it off, didn't even dare throw it in the wastebasket, tore it into tiny pieces and put it into the chemical toilet. He was literally afraid that this little piece of paper and the carelessness of the kidnappers who had left it there could cost him his life, if they noticed that he had seen it. The next bottle had a sticker, too. He took that one off as well. As subsequent bottles also had stickers, he gradually got used to the idea that the kidnappers apparently didn't care if he knew where they did their shopping. This idea gave him a new fright.

There was another risk in the short exchanges with the Englishman, if they went any further than simple questions on his part and the relevant answers. Naturally he wanted to find out what he could about the kidnappers, to learn a little more about his situation and his chances. And also, just to talk to someone. Fundamentally, he wanted to be a real person in the Englishman's mind, not just an object of exchange. This was, as far as he could see, the only thing he could do for his own survival: work toward the unlikely but possible moment when the Englishman would face the decision of whether to kill him or not—and might not be sure which way he should go. He wanted to do all he could to prepare for this extremity, to sway things somewhat in his favor, which is why he wanted the Englishman to feel his subjective essence. He tried to avoid all submissiveness and all aggressiveness in his language, since both of these arouse aggression. He tried to be polite, to accept as an unquestioned aspect of their conversations the kidnappers' premise that "it's only business," without subordinating himself to them completely: "It's your business, but it's my life." But, to avoid any false impressions: how convincing the utterances were that resulted from these calculations of his, I cannot say. Twice in conversations with the Englishman he came close to tears, once over the demand that his wife act as money carrier, and another time after one of the failed transfers. Whatever the reason, the risk inherent in these conversations was that he would induce the Englishman to say things that he might decide afterward were too revealing. There were a few interesting questions he asked, but only later; once or twice he said, "I want to ask you something, but please don't give me an answer you would regret afterward." What he meant was "an answer *I* would regret."

Several times he wondered about asking the Englishman to undo the chain. But he didn't do it. Such a request would have contained an unspoken reference to his good conduct (under duress, but nonetheless demonstrated) up until now, and this went against his grain. Once, however, when the chain had been taken off for a few minutes so that he could change sweat suits, and was being reattached, he asked, "Do you think you need the chain anymore?" Answer: "Yes, because there isn't always someone upstairs." This made him think that perhaps he might be able to break the door down from the inside.

Of course, he kept imagining how he might free himself, even if these thoughts didn't get him very far, since it was pointless to think about the door or the (apparently) two windows. The question was whether he could free the chain, i.e., whether he could manage to dislodge the dowelling that held it in the wall. How deep did it go? It couldn't be moved, but the plaster itself was quite soft. So how thick was the layer of plaster? What was behind it? Bricks? Cement? He couldn't find out, because any halfhearted or serious attempt to do so would, if discovered, incur the threatened consequences. He was afraid that any traces of activity around the place where the chain was fixed into the wall would lead to sanctions. The chain, as he had already discovered, played a decisive role in the kidnappers' security system.

But how would he have set to work in the event that something could have been done at the wall? First of all, he had nothing but the plastic cutlery. The most he could have done with this was scratch a little at the plaster.

Would it be possible to break the plastic chair? Hardly. It was rigid, but tough. One evening when his breakfast plate (hard plastic) had not been removed because he had left some bread on it uneaten, he hid it. The Englishman soon noticed it was missing and did a superficial search, but didn't seem interested after that (it would surely turn up again). Later on, when they supplemented the water in plastic bottles (which were useless for his purposes) with fruit juice that came in glass bottles, he set an empty one aside. They let it stay there for a day; then, after a conversation with the Englishman, it was gone. He hid the next one under the old newspapers, which were never cleared out. Over time, he raised this to three bottles. How far he would get with them, of course, he had no idea. But he would have to try. If he failed, he would save a suitable broken piece for killing himself. The washbasin would help, because he could lay his slashed wrist in the water, which would speed the bleeding. On the other hand, the water could also function as drinking water, which might help him survive a bit longer. When he heard the news afterward that when one of the kidnappers was arrested, he had tried to slit his wrists, he was filled with a sense of satisfaction.

"There is no word I know of in the German language to describe the feeling one has after being kidnapped. A sense of deathly aloneness has to be dismantled bit by bit. One is shamed by the force of hatred that overwhelms all one's carefully nurtured civilized instincts" is what one letter said that I received after my kidnapping. The person who wrote it is not someone who would have formulated such an observation lightly. The man speaking here of his shame over the force of his own hatred is someone who went through much worse than I did, yet I cannot align his view of the world with my own, or take his attitude as an example I can follow. I respect it, I admire the strength it took to get that far—but I could not summon up such strength if I wanted to. But I am only ashamed of those hours—of too many of them—when I did not hate, because I wasn't strong enough to do so. I remember vividly his self-disgust when he felt happy to hear the Englishman's voice, just because it was a human voice, a human voice and part of the world external to the cellar which was detached from that world altogether.

An old idea from childhood: what would happen if I could make myself invisible? Or: what would happen if I could make time stop? He would love to have slammed the Englishman's head against the wall. And then wrapped the chain around his neck. No, he should be able to get air, but the chain should be tight. He also wondered whether to extend the chain to his feet so that his whole body was pulled backward like a bow—but he abandoned that. But he would leave him in the dark. Water within reach, yes. And he would let time go by. Not a very long time, but more than would be necessary to alert the police. He wanted to instill a maximum of fear in a limited period, but without overstepping certain bounds, to stop before reaching a place, even in his fantasies, where unbridled hatred could take him. No complete abandonment of conduct becoming a gentleman. Was he following the image of the Englishman he had created for himself? Or was private revenge just not what he wanted? If this had happened to his wife or son instead of him, he would have wanted it. Had he allowed himself to think about *this* in a little more detail (which he forbade himself to do in the fiercest terms), he would have drowned for a time in fantasies of an orgy of violence. Things being the way they were, what he wanted above all was to see the criminals facing a courtroom. Not just know it was happening; *see* it. He wanted to see them at last, and was happy to delegate his actual retaliation to others. (Once outside the cellar, after I had been plied liberally by the media with pictures of some of the criminals, this wish took a backseat. Now I am no longer interested in how the scum look. I just want to know they're behind bars.)

If it came to that, how would he talk to the court? His treatment at their hands would be a subject that might affect the severity of the sentence. He the kidnap victim, he whom they had thrown headfirst against a wall, tied up, gagged, loaded into a car all covered in blood, and transported who knew where, he would have to give evidence to the court as a witness to the relative humanity of the man who had organized it all. He worked out for himself in the cellar that this would not upset him. What had happened had happened, and in no other way. That is what he would say—the truth and nothing but the truth. And what had happened to the hatred? I have no choice but to deal quite comprehensively with something that is much less pleasant to explore than fantasies of hatred (even those a lot grimmer than his own), namely his positive feelings for his kidnappers.

These feelings are known as the "Stockholm syndrome," after a hostage-taking in Stockholm during which the relationship between hostages and captors became almost friendly. This concept had been detached from its original setting to describe—or at least label—a more general condition. An aggravating, often embarrassing one. The relationship of hostages with hostage-takers, i.e., with those who are threatening their lives, who have beaten and hurt them, who are responsible for the fear of death the hostages must endure, and who are the cause of all the terror visited on the people against whom the blackmail is being directed, is often too close to be acceptable in a civilized world. He already had an inkling in his cellar that this could possibly become the greatest hindrance to what is usually termed the "working through" of the event, if he were to survive, and I can confirm it. I was compelled to keep coming back to it in the first weeks after his release; I talked about it all the time, kept thinking about it, made jokes and got on my wife's nerves to a notable extent. She did not like these little snippets of everyday life in the cellar.

For those who are uninvolved, they are the seasoning in the anecdotal soup. Tales from Nowhere. Amazing, bizarre details. And the person telling them becomes their star. The press loves hearing them and spreads them. This gives rise to a false picture of the cellar and of the person who found himself there, even if it may be flattering to me. In a letter I received after his release, it said: ". . . From what the newspapers say, you are confronting the wounding of your sense of self-worth and integrity both directly and with irony, and I see from this that you gave no ground to your captors, either implicitly or explicitly." Nice if it were true.

Let us take the situation the evening before the last ransom handover. The longer his time in the cellar went on, the greater the part that chance began to play in his fantasies and fears. He noticed that, like many people presumably, he had lived until now in the unconscious assumption that his life was following a script in which certain things would simply never happen, at least not things like this violent intrusion from outside, this reduction to goods or exchange for cash; it was also becoming increasingly clear to him that he now found himself caught up in something in which intentions were not the only deciding factor. Anything was possible, not just the act of will exercised by his kidnappers but *any thing*. It was possible not only that the police might hold his life to be less important than the capture of the perpetrators, it was possible not only that the police might make mistakes that could cost him his life, that ordinary people searching for him could be assumed by the kidnappers to be the police, it was also possible that some perfectly normal, uniformed, and uninformed police patrol could burst into the middle of one of the money transfers. Or something could happen either on the side of the money carriers or on that of the kidnappers that was completely unforeseen. Car accidents, for example. "If we don't come back, no one will release you."

So he saw his kidnappers at three in the morning, somewhere south of Münster, with thirty million Deutsche marks in the car, euphoric but nerve-jangled, on their way to an interim hiding place for the money. Two seconds asleep at the wheel, a guard rail, the car spins, an oncoming truck, broken necks, blood, fire, singed bank notes blowing around the highway. Time passes. Perhaps there is something announced on the radio, perhaps not, perhaps it's irrelevant. In any case, no one comes back. An agreed time of return, of which he knows nothing down in the cellar, expires. The person upstairs probably waits a bit longer, since she doesn't want to believe in a bad ending, either, and will give fate another chance. Then a feeling of her own endangerment will gain the upper hand, and she will leave. Time will pass, it's 9, 10, 11 a.m. (they had told him it could take that long). Then noon, 1, 2 p.m. When would he decide that the thing he dreaded more than anything else had happened? When would fear of a very slow death in the cellar become stronger than the fear of the kidnappers suddenly coming in to make good on their threat to render the conditions of his imprisonment unendurable? When, after all attempts to free himself had proved pointless, would the hope of being found become smaller than the aversion to the moment when he would have to grapple seriously with the question of where best to apply the broken piece of glass? These feelings and thoughts led him to talk to the Englishman as he was leaving for what might be the last round in the game as if he were a worried mother, on the one hand because, like a worried mother, he didn't want to leave anything unsaid, although, also like a worried mother, he knew that in case of doubt, such warnings are useless, and on the other hand because he felt he had to put his fear into words so as not to choke on it, that he wanted to give it form and substance without allowing its full extent to become apparent to the person who was the cause and source of all fear and all hope—in short, he said: "Drive carefully."

The absurdity of these two words did not escape him. He added (naturally the intellectual in him didn't want to disappear completely in this mishmash of anxiety): "That's what they call the Stockholm syndrome." The Englishman laughed. Professionals together. And he did feel better after these two sentences, and this fact requires attention.

Whenever he managed to give substance to a feeling (usually in the form of a few sentences in his diary), he felt better. It wasn't that this enabled him to conquer the feeling or take hold of it, just that—however this might be expressed—he wasn't so exposed to it. Or perhaps I should say: he wasn't exposed *in* it. Writing marked a place outside feeling, and in writing he controlled this place. It was a form of self-defense against the reduction of the world to any overwhelming feeling. It was somewhat the same when he spoke, but unlike the act of writing, his conversation could not contain as its subject his actual feelings. When he wanted to address them, he did so indirectly, transposing them into a problem. He disguised his fear of death in an effort to get them to understand the tactics of those left at home: "Of course, they are afraid that you will kill me as soon as you get the money." Of course, they were his wife, his son—who told him later they hadn't believed they would see him again ("People are kidnapped, they pay, and then they're killed anyway")—the police. But he too. The sentence "We won't hurt you, it's just business," which he heard on the very second day, relieved him somewhat, but did nothing to convince him, not in a way he could rely on, that he was going to come out of it alive. So he was relieved for a second time when the Englishman said, in answer to his bid for understanding, that there had never been a case of a hostage being murdered after the payment of a really high ransom, "The police know, your lawyer knows, and they will tell your wife." And he counted off the names: Albrecht, Oetker, Snoek. It became clear that the Englishman wanted to calm him, too: "If they pay, we won't kill you. I promise."

He did not ask whether they would in fact kill him later, if the next money transfer failed, or the one after that. He didn't want to hear the answer, since it could only be yes, even in the unlikely event that his kidnappers had given up by then. A hostage who had the feeling that, regardless of the outcome of the extortion, nothing was going to happen to him would be of no use to them when it came to writing further letters. And once, unasked, the Englishman had said, "We won't give up."

It was the conversations as such that brought relief. It was the cliché that is also real (as clichés so often are): at least a human voice. In all the thirty-three days, he had perhaps a total of one hour of conversation with the Englishman. These short conversations, or rather exchanges, were oases in the monotony. Sometimes he learned something to do with the outside. Most often something he would rather not have known, but the thick end of the wedge, so to speak, came afterward; during the conversation itself it was the blessing of talking that defined the mood. I am not exaggerating when I use the word "blessing." He liked this voice. He found it appealing. And he could analyze the feeling; it was not one he found pleasant, but he could not hold it at a distance. He liked the fact that the voice spoke English. He sometimes had to search for words, which prolonged the conversation, and he could sometimes work something out in advance. English allows you to be succinct, ironic, sarcastic, and yet not so immediately cynical as German. He sometimes had the feeling that the idiom itself obliged him not to become too self-pitying. Sometimes, when he couldn't resist the temptation (he always tried not to give in to it) to imagine what it would be like when he was free again, what he would tell to whom, and how, he began involuntarily to think in English.

How far did all this go? Far. He once had the fantasy that the kidnapper should be comforting him, touching him, laying a hand on his shoulder. It is not easy for me to write this; it was not easy for him to admit to this desire, because the feeling cannot be equated with a human voice that one longs to hear, no matter whose it is. Not even the voice was that simple. But the desire for physical contact crossed the line into submission. There is no ambiguity in a power relationship—no division of power, just a crass juxtaposition of all-powerfulness and powerlessness—and the powerless one, the one who has been "overpowered," wishes for the gift of bodily contact from the one who holds the power. Even the fantasy of a hand on the shoulder is extreme.

It distinguishes itself from any exchange of words in that it is not subject to irony. The self-commentary and self-distancing in a sentence such as "That's what they call the Stockholm syndrome" are nowhere to be found in the fantasy about the hand. Which is why this fantasy marks a psychological nadir that he experienced at that moment and which I do not wish to gloss over. If the Englishman on his side had wanted to establish a closeness, as in the sentence "You want to get out of here, and we have no interest in holding you here any longer—we're in the same boat," he in turn could have savored this closeness, which remained verbal (and which signaled to him that he had a chance of surviving this nightmare), while recognizing the fact of it and simultaneously keeping his distance from it by answering, "Yes, but you chose it."

Autonomy would naturally be an inapposite word for someone at the end of a chain, yet he was able to salvage a fragment of the idea of personal autonomy in a few sentences over the course of the days. But I am not deceiving myself: these exchanges had some undertone of buddies together, something almost cronyish about them. My wife, as I've said, did not like these stories of his about the cellar. They struck her as *too* anecdotal. I think it was this moment of male bonding that, to her, marked a crossing of the boundaries of extreme power. A tiny snapshot from the world that Sam Peckinpah captures in *The Wild Bunch*.

How his wife would have behaved in his place was not something he ever wondered about in the cellar. He forbade himself to think that this could have happened to his wife or his son. And so he also avoided thinking about how he would behave if he were on the outside. When the Englishman wanted to find out if it really had been his wife, as opposed to a police psychologist, on the other end of the telephone, and—as already recounted—said that the voice had not been timid but amazingly aggressive, did this sound like her? He not only had no need to pretend with the Englishman but was almost as happy as if he had been able to hear her himself. In her place, would he have been imperious to the Englishman, or would he have taken a factual, businesslike tone? He would not have sounded pleading, because he would have been held back by the idea that such behavior was simply false. But this is not the question. For the person on the outside, the kidnapper is an abstract threat with a few random traits—bizarre when viewed in isolation—such as accent, choice of words, gestures of brutality. For the kidnap victim, the kidnapper is the sole reality aside from the cell itself—at least the only one with which any contact can be made, about which (perhaps) it is worth thinking, the only one that may (perhaps again) be open to influence. The only human being within reach.

You are never free of the thought: This man has my life at his disposal. In two respects: he can kill me at any time (and it can be assumed that he will do so if it seems to him advantageous, out of some calculation I can only partially guess at), and for as long as I remain alive, the conditions of my life depend on him alone.

And "conditions of life" is a phrase to be pondered in such a context.

Two and a half weeks after my release, I dreamed that I was being shot. I tried to save my life by talking, but it was hopeless, I had seen his face. (It was not the Englishman, to whom I had avoided giving a face in the dream, it was someone else; it was also not a reprise of the actual abduction but a repetition of a situation which had been feared, anticipated, and expected so many times before). I didn't know when it would happen, only that it would be soon. I was reading a book, *Danton's Death,* and in it the names of Damien and St. Preux; so this was an allusion to the whole span of violent death from the endless agony of those tortured slowly and publicly to death, to the guillotine, to suicide. Then I was shot from behind in the head. A blow, not painful, a feeling of something being torn out of my skull, parts of my brain spattered on the book in front of me, and simultaneously the thought "I'm not dead, he aimed badly, I hope he shoots again so that it's over"; a second shot—I think that I am still thinking, but the thought gets fainter, or smaller, and disappears. Blackness.

In the cellar he often thought about what it might be like, would be like, if they shot him. He thought it was possible; the hope of "If they pay, we won't kill you, I promise" might be real, but he could never fully rely on it, to feel truly safe. Only when the Englishman let go of his hand in the wood and told him he could take off the blindfold now and start walking straight ahead did he say to himself, "I really am going to survive this." All the statistics—so horribly contradicted in the months after his release but still valid in March–April 1996—according to which such kidnappings end without the murder of the victim if the ransom is paid could not divert him from the fact that up until a certain moment he was worth twenty, later thirty million marks, and that once that moment had passed he was a not very dangerous, but equally not undangerous witness. And what would happen if further handovers went wrong? When would the kidnappers decide that the risks attendant on yet another attempt were too great? They must know very well that each time, they left traces behind, no matter how minuscule, and that their odds were not improving.

How fast do you die when you're shot in the head? Fast, he supposed, which is why he hoped that if they killed him, that would be how they did it. He also hoped that they would tell him shortly before they did it. Not a long time before, for he had no desire to wait as if in a death cell (although he sometimes had the feeling that he was on death row, but only the feeling, not the certainty), but it shouldn't just happen from one moment to the next. He did not want the last sensation in his life to be a sudden fear or horror. If it had to happen, he wanted to experience something like the dignity of an execution. Is that the right word? Should I say "stage"? But it was hardly in his power to stage anything. No, he wanted to say something before he was shot. No—no kitsch about last words in willful obliviousness of the circumstances and under some delusion that the world would hear him. And not to tell the kidnappers anything to their faces or to impress them somehow with his manly steadfastness. None of that, since fear had not reduced him to complete idiocy. He wanted the last sound in his ear to be his own voice, he wanted to close out his life himself. The last things should not be dizziness and terror but this tiny bit of sovereignty and autonomy that can be preserved in a final sentence.

But being shot is simply one possibility. Strangely, he never once thought about being killed in some other way. How real such a possibility was has become clear in the meantime. What he did always expect, however, was that they would just leave him in the cellar. His chances of freeing himself or being discovered in time, if their intention was to let him die of thirst, were, he assumed, very small—as I later had to recognize, exactly nil. So the kidnappers, personified by the Englishman, were not only lords of life and death but also lords of the manner of his death, which could either be more or less quick and (relatively) painless, or slow and terrible. They were also lords of his life until that point (or until his release), and this command over all conditions of life was one that allowed any excess. Time could stretch on just as it had until now. He would get water and food, make his own decision about whether his cell would be dark or lit; he would be able to wash himself, clean his teeth, comb his hair, use a toilet. He would be able to read and write, and also receive newspapers and, periodically, information about how negotiations were proceeding. Or they could disconnect the light, discontinue or considerably reduce his care, tie him up, gag him, and just leave him lying there for hours or days. They could mutilate him, as they had threatened. They had the power to do anything to him that came into their heads. That they had not so far shown themselves to be the type of kidnappers who are sadistic, who relish their own absolute power and choose to demonstrate its lack of limits to themselves and their victim by their excesses, did not mean that all this might not change—perhaps due to rising exasperation. And: were all the participants alike? There could be two factions, and the balance of power in the group could shift if the "soft-line" proponents had no success. What if the kidnappers decided that his letters were too controlled and too calm? What if they decided he was simply not alarmed enough? What if their rising nervousness and anger began to seek an outlet? And so on. They held all the power and freedom in relation to him, he had none, discounting the fact that after a certain point he had the power to commit suicide. Thanks to the broken piece of glass from one of the bottles he had saved. Cassius's lines from *Julius Caesar* about the power of the weak ran again and again through his head, but the question amounted to pathetic attitudinizing in the wrong place, for the possibility of suicide was bound up with his changeable situation in the cellar. If he were to be tied up, it would be impossible, and the act of collecting the bottles increased this very risk. He simply relied on the fact that the cellar would not be searched because nobody had searched it thus far, and he was right.

Whoever is in a situation in which literally anything can happen to him because he is powerless and others have absolute power over him should thank his lucky stars if he never has to learn what absolute power actually can be. But he will always experience his fate in the person of whoever holds the power over him. He will be grateful to this person, as the embodiment of his fate, for everything that does not happen to him. He will be grateful for being allowed to keep his watch, so that he can divide the day into morning, noon, afternoon, evening, and night. For being able to feel that the day has a regular course, instead of having the sensation of not even swimming but treading water in undifferentiated, empty time. He will be grateful for light, for water, for food. When his request for reading matter was fulfilled not just by another delivery of newspapers but by the first group of books, and then, even more unexpectedly, by the second, he couldn't hold back his tears. Tears of relief and gratitude. He had forbidden himself tears until then. Had always imagined the moment when he would come home and take his wife and his son in his arms, so that he could then collapse, release the tension, weep. He betrayed this vision for a plastic bag of books and a feeling of gratitude toward a man who not only had beaten and abducted, chained and imprisoned him but also was terrorizing his family and keeping his thirteen-year-old son in a state in which he had no idea whether he would ever see his father alive again.

And yet nothing is more unremarkable than this betrayal. He had every reason for gratitude. How he would have endured darkness and the absence of anything to read for weeks on end was something he didn't know, and I don't know the answer today, either. With the books, he knew he had a chance. And more: getting hold of them raised the risks for the kidnappers, only a fraction, but somewhat nonetheless. Yet they brought or bought him some all the same. Why? Out of some impulse that, however inappropriate it sounds in this context, could be called humanity? They were coldhearted criminals, but not boundlessly malevolent, or at least did not wish to appear to be, whether by impulse or by calculation, and this circumstance stamped thirty-three days of his life that could have been his last if things had been otherwise, or thirty-three days that could have sent him back into life more damaged in body and soul than they did. He had reason to be grateful.

This feeling contradicted his hate, and frequently his self-respect. It was something to be kept at a distance and analyzed. It was important to recognize what caused it, to know that it was not insane, that it simply corresponded to the insanity of a situation in which one person was omnipotent and the other helpless. And it must never be allowed to obliterate the fact of what the criminals had done. He had to stop himself from falling in with the logic of "We're all in the same

boat" without adding the corrective "But you chose it."
He helped himself by making a distinction: however
the relationship between him and the criminals (read:
the Englishman) would eventually appear, whether he
would want to say to the court that things had been
relatively tolerable for him and personally he did not
harbor continuing resentment over the time that had
been stolen from him—what they had done to his family was something he would never forgive. This was no
mental game. He had only to turn his thoughts from
the cellar toward home, and he felt nothing but helpless rage.

Naturally, any feeling that corresponds to the objective insanity of a situation is itself insane. The insanity
possesses the person subjected to it. It is hard to free
yourself from this insanity, and time has made clear to
me that this perfectly comprehensible and objectively
reasonable feeling of sympathy with the criminals is
not the least of what they have done to me. It is like a
rape, and the loss of the capacity to be able to hate on
one's own behalf amounts to a deformation of the psyche. (I say "capacity." As regards the individual will to
overcome hate, let everyone exercise the values he or
she recognizes. But to decide to forgo hate presup-
poses that there is an *option* to decide otherwise.)

Moreover, it was not "comparatively tolerable." For
the record, I must categorically contradict what was
sometimes in his feelings. It is incredibly hard to
feel your way back into certain states of fear when
everything is apparently behind you. There is a wall
that separates you from these feelings. You cannot

climb over it, you also cannot stand on top of it and gain perspective. Yet there are moments when it can disappear. You need such moments if you want to look back at the states of extreme experience, but the problem is that you don't want to. Nobody wants to go back to the cellar.

There's another part of this. It is painful to write about your own fear when its causes are not so immediately obvious. People warned my son about watching the video of a reenactment of my abduction—it was supposed to be very brutal. I don't know to what extent my son had imagined his way into the scene in front of our house (aside from his flattering [to me] insinuation that the blood might not be mine, but from one of the kidnappers), but compared with the reality, this re-enacted ambush was a piece of harmless theater. The harmless variety is already quite extreme enough. Nonetheless, the dramatic high points of the story have no trouble touching the imagination and fears of all those watching and listening. The normality of what I call one's kidnapping (or kidnapped) day eludes all fellow feeling.

Two reactions are typical. One can be summed up in the question of how one can endure such a time of imprisonment at all. The other expresses the view that nothing short of bloodshed and starvation counts, or at least is really not worth mentioning. This latter makes good use of the quote about the "deluxe kidnapping," "a definition that Reemtsma openly shares," as one newspaper said. An even clearer demonstration was the version of his story current in the press which drew

on a remark by a police spokesman during a press conference: "When Mr. Reemtsma knocked, one of his
kidnappers would come to ask what he wanted." Here
the disappointment that he was not further brutalized
after his abduction and that he got through thirty-
three days without losing his common sense or his
mind combines with what people would probably
think of Mr. Reemtsma anyway: that someone like *him*
would only have to knock for a person to come and ask
what they could do for him.

Even if the second reaction can be explained reas-
suringly by reference to Pavlov, the first question—of
how it could be endured at all—is more complicated.

It provokes a counterquestion: What makes you
think I did endure it? Or: What do you mean by "did
not endure"? Where is the dividing line between
enduring and not enduring? I could just as easily say,
on the basis of his experiences, that enduring thirty-
three days is not so hard as all that. He and I did not
endure it at all. This is because the fact or the mental
construct of utter powerlessness seems to be bound
up with an idea of a moment when you simply give up.
But if someone gives up, the only difference between
this and carrying on is that the person with all the
power notices.

His exercise of power must also factor in the point
when the victim gives up. This sometimes happens
during torture (but appallingly enough, less often than
is assumed). In the case of hostage-taking, this point
usually does not occur at all. The hostage has neither
the choice of fleeing or standing his ground, nor of

standing his ground or supporting the goals of the hostage-takers. He is completely dependent on others. His state of mind, his self-image, what he wants to say, his feelings, his desires, how he changes, whether he wants to cry out in fear or whether he clenches his teeth, whether he goes nuts or counts, step after step, in the course of a day, to 18,500, is all completely irrelevant. How did he endure it? Was there anything he was not allowed to have done, for people to be able to say he endured it? What is someone imagining who says with conviction, "*I* would not have endured that"?

A likelihood that something gives out. Someone endures, and then endures no longer. And then? Then the confession, if a confession is what's wanted. Or a scream that replaces the teeth clenched together to stifle a scream. But what if there is no such point set either by oneself or someone else? In his cellar he often had the feeling that he wanted to give up; he also felt it was equally unfair that he had no chance to give up and thus to effect something. Both the possibility of giving up and the possibility of not giving up, but actively enduring, had been taken from him. He was not faced with any choice at all. No one demanded of him that he denounce someone else, which he could have refused. No one demanded that he renounce a belief, so he had no opportunity to stand fast. Not that he regretted it. He didn't have many illusions, and had never supposed himself to be a particularly courageous man, more the kind who gives up as soon as he is shown the instruments. But the way things were, all that was at issue here was his life on the one hand or a very great deal of money on the other. He was an object of exchange, with no role as a protagonist. He was thus robbed of all spiritual resources from which he might otherwise have drawn strength. It doesn't matter a jot whether he behaved submissively or arrogantly, whether he wept or not, whether he came to terms with the idea that tomorrow he would be dead, or considered this attitude a scandal.

It did of course play a role in his sense of self; it was perhaps not *entirely* irrelevant to his relationship with his captors, but nonetheless it remains true that during his kidnapping such questions simply did not arise.

Besides, he could do nothing to assist his release. Well, he certainly could have tried to overpower his guards, but in order to do so he would have had to be out of his mind. He was chained up, his guards were professional thugs, possibly armed, and seemed to come mostly in pairs—certainly whenever his chain was being removed. He could only wait and hope that his wife, the people helping her on the outside, the police would do the right thing. He could only wait until it pleased other people to let him out again. The only thing he could do at some point was to choose new people to deliver the ransom money, and this meant exposing people to a risk which he himself could only estimate in a very limited way. He could only wait and know that other people might be risking their lives for him. His great sense of gratitude is always accompanied by feelings of shame and guilt.

Perhaps being overpowered is always accompanied by feelings of shame. My wife has told me that she felt shamed by the sight of the hand grenade on the extortion letter, and by the "confession" to others that I had been kidnapped. Being overpowered makes you small, reduces you, hands you over, is a continual violation and humiliation, even when there is apparently nothing embarrassing for those who stand outside it. The effect is that you always believe you have some part in the blame. In the sense that this kidnapping could have been avoided with the effort of a little foresight, or the people who planned it could have been shown the pointlessness of their plan, that through my own neglect I therefore share responsibility for the difficulties the crime caused other people, particularly for the worry and suffering of my family. But no one should carry such thoughts too far, however correct they may be. The person who is guilty of a crime is the person who committed it, not the person upon whom it was committed.

That guilt can declare itself so insistently in tandem with shame is a result of the difficulty mentioned earlier of coming to terms in one's heart with a sudden irruption of force. The most frightening idea of evil is not that of the wicked demon but that of God playing like a child. It is easier to accept an evil fate than sheer chance. You hear people whose lives have taken a bad turn often complaining that they have done nothing to deserve it and asking what they could have done wrong. It is usually simpler to accept an injustice than a world that is not organized according to any measure of justice and injustice or at least right and wrong.

Thus the feeling of shame unleashed by an over-whelming assault is often accompanied by guilt, be-cause one can use it to block out a fuller insight into the arbitrary tyranny of the event.

Confronted with this arbitrary force in such an extreme way, one also recognizes just how much one might have assumed up until that point that one was in control of one's own life. His having to say to him-self again and again during the attack and on the jour-ney to their hiding place and in the first days thereafter that this really was reality was because he had to im-pose this awareness of reality on a strange sensation of inappropriateness. He had to work to convince himself that his life could come to an end from one moment to the next, for like most people he tended always to view the present from the perspective of an anticipated future, and now had to tell himself that there was some likelihood this future would not exist.

So even fear has to be *learned,* i.e., not just *experi-enced* as a destructive presence, but as a feeling corre-sponding to reality. But this did not enable him to keep it at a distance. Whenever I talked with my wife about our thirty-three days, but particularly when I read the notes she kept about them, it became clear to me what lay at the heart of the difference in our two situations. It is *not* what seems at first to be obvious, that the one is held captive and sees his life threatened, whereas the other can act—and must, because the life of the prisoner depends on her. As different as these roles are, the feelings they engendered were often very much the same. Except in one fundamental way: feelings of fear, helplessness, hope, expectation, etc., outside the cellar were connected with particular social relationships and situations. Discussion of the circumstances generating fear or hope, his son's expression as he tries, at age thirteen, to conceal his alarm, the afterthoughts about whether it was or will be right or wrong to have done or do this or that, the loneliness finally, the feeling of having to rely only on oneself—this is what points up the difference. The lonelinesses outside the cellar were the absences of other people; the loneliness in the cellar had nothing whatever in common with that. My wife could miss me—in the place where she herself was. He could not have the reciprocal feeling. Outside the cellar was a structure of human relationships and communication that had had to absorb disruption and destruction and now had to adapt itself to the new situation. In the cellar he had fallen out of the network of all real human communication, if one ignores the brief conversational exchanges and the fact that he was compelled in his own mind to create and then occupy some zone where he could accommodate himself to the tension between total power and total powerlessness. His feelings were unquestionably "his," but because there was no feedback, their content existed only in his imagination. Feelings such as those in the cellar do not result from the relation someone like my wife has to others or to me in my absence, but are there, break in, just as THAT broke in, and require psychological definition. Just as he was "out of the world," his feelings were not "of this world" but feelings in the cellar, which he could only comprehend by dint of comparisons, or sometimes simulations. That was why his greatest fear was always the continuation of this condition, not—which may surprise many people who have never been in the cellar—the fear of mutilation, and not even the fear of death.

Four and a half weeks of the fear of death. That is what seems to be the easiest to adjust to, for almost everyone is afraid of death. Is also afraid of dying, as I have already described. But that wasn't the worst. When he wrote that the safest thing was to agree to the kidnappers' terms, he did not know whether he was right, and he was aware of this. But he wanted it finally to come to an end. It was a lottery game and he wanted to wager on this possibility without ifs or buts. If it was a no-win game, okay; if not, not. There were not a few hours when it seemed to him more bearable to be shot than to go on waiting for weeks and weeks. It would not have been that way if they had presented him with the alternative, given him the *choice* between death and, let's say, months or years to go. Then he could have decided (could know there would be an end, and wait for it). He could have resolved to endure, if not for himself, then for his family. But those were not his circumstances in the cellar. I do not think I can make it believable to anyone who has not been through something similar that the truly terrible thing is *the absolute helplessness,* the being-delivered-over to other people. A part of one's humanness is canceled out by it that otherwise remains whole even in death, because before death it is possible to fantasize about what is beyond dying. Whoever makes a will exercises control beyond death, he is, at least in his own anticipatory fantasy, "there" beyond death. Whoever is completely impotent is no longer "there" even in a living body. In addition, he had no idea—given the rules of the game—where he was. He was simply gone, even for those on the outside who were thinking about him. Where were they supposed to imagine him? Under what conditions? And he fantasized their fantasies—and stopped himself. This feeling of no longer being there, of being reduced to a thing, is not some kind of insult because one has lost the capacity to feel it as such. Dealing with it should be a small matter, like learning to live with the chain.

A newspaper said that he had been held in the cellar "like an animal." Indeed, but an insult is something against which the autonomous subjective self rises in fury, against which one can rebel or summon up revenge fantasies. It is precisely those capacities that are required to perceive an insult which are the ones to be damaged in a situation like his, and this is why things from this point on are no longer communicable. I know that anyone who has been through something like this will understand me. Everyone else will have to take my word for it. There are feelings—and they declare themselves unmistakably both psychologically and bodily—which cannot be measured against what passes for unpleasantness in the everyday world. It is not "that and that, just worse." It is quite *other*.

In the cellar he came to see that something I had long considered to be theoretically questionable but historically interesting, namely the concept of the "individual" as the representation of a human being in whom some continuity and stability holds true in the face of all life's vicissitudes, was completely obsolete. I received a well-intentioned letter on this theme: in these circumstances, "to have retained one's individuality" was worthy of particular recognition. If I reject these friendly lines, it is not out of modesty but out of my self-observation in the cellar.

In one of the books the kidnappers had brought him, he had stumbled upon the following sentence from St. Augustine: "Nole foras ire, in te ipsum redi; in interiore homine habitat veritas; et si tuam naturam mutabilem inveneris, transcende et te ipsum" (Do not go outward, go into yourself; truth dwells in the heart of man; and when you have recognized your nature in its inconstancy, transcend even yourself). There are sentences that are read until they start giving up the wrong meaning. But beyond that, this sentence is interesting because it contains both a normal misunderstanding and an irritation derived from self-observation. The misunderstanding comes from assuming that there is something like a kernel in the human soul that is called "I." If one goes into oneself seriously enough, one bumps into this "I," and it is this "I" that also remains the same throughout one's life. One never steps into the same river twice, but he who steps into it is supposed to remain the same. And why does he remain the same? Because this "I" exists. In situations of extremity, this "I" is the crucible. If body and soul are abused, it also suffers wounds, but at the end it has survived and everyone can say "He has stayed the same despite everything." The idea of such an "I" also allows of a connection to the idea of "enduring." One has endured "it," whatever "it" may be, if the kernel of the human being has survived undamaged. You come out of the cellar like Alec Guinness as an English officer coming out of a Japanese prison cage; as the person you were. Applause.

Western philosophy—for historical reasons which need not be gone into here—is driven by this problem. The search is always for the inner core, which, when I have found it, is also my point of departure for the external world, a core which may be completely uncertain, may even be partially illusion, but which should nonetheless contain some fixed and reliable element: my "I." Augustine's introspection finds no such appropriate element. Everything within is far too diffuse, unstable, exposed to outside impressions to lend itself to the Archimedean point. It is interesting that this finding (or this failure of the attempt to find something) does not cause any disquiet, but for Augustine just shows how greatly mankind needs God, since mankind cannot find sufficient purchase and security within itself. The Archimedean point for him must lie outside the world, but that is naturally a Christian *façon de parler*. What is meant is the congregation that Augustine in his fantasy of God's State wishes to become a mighty fortress such as Rome never was and Plato's Republic never could be.

Descartes poses Augustine's question again, and answers it differently: the "I" for him *is* the departure point for everything else. With it he founds the mainstream of modern European philosophy, and its related dissenters—Montaigne, let's say, or David Hume—remain on the margins. If, without describing the potential philosophical curve, I contrast this with my feelings in the cellar, I have to admit that the Cartesian search was not successful. (Ironically, the four hundredth anniversary of the birth of Descartes fell during his time in the cellar, and he had the opportunity of reading several truly awful newspaper supplements produced for the occasion.)

When he wasn't distracting himself by reading or writing, he was exposed to his feelings, and I cannot begin to employ any of the images that are conventionally applied to such states, such as a ship in a storm. He *was* his feelings, and nothing could have mastered them—not because whatever was there was too weak, but because there was simply nothing there. The feeling that must be present to enable someone to use the first person singular without awkwardness (whatever this feeling may be called: individuality or identity or authenticity) requires a complex relationship to the external world, to objects as much as to other human beings. Social relationships, communication, some minimal exercise of power over things must all exist. This is also why communication with the person who represents power takes on particularly humiliating significance for the one who is powerless; and why the rituals of storing things up, the expertise about the chain, which in retrospect give rise to a kind of pathetic veteran's pride, become so important. And also why the achievement of the means to commit suicide is such a triumph. They are mechanisms of a personality structure which has grown out of the European habit of perceiving oneself as an individual, which talks to itself as "I," and which encounters existential problems when it is detached from the social context that is essential to it.

An internal process requires external criteria—this sentence of Wittgenstein's referring to the possibility of understanding other people's feelings also holds true for oneself. These external criteria can of course be projected onto an Augustinian God (or any other), they can be an imaginary afterworld. It is possible to achieve such mental projections. He could only do so in the cellar in a very limited way. He could not build himself a "prison identity" out of his situation with the chain like some kind of toy, nor could he fantasize himself as some kind of martyr. He was in the cellar because of his money, and money on its own is useless for the building of an identity and those ardent feelings which are necessary to the marshaling of psychic resources in the face of a demeaning, potentially murderous situation. Things really would have been different if the cause of his abduction had been a political one that had something to do with him as a political person. Again: it would certainly have been more dangerous, more brutal, more painful, but it would also have been different. To use Sartre's terminology, he would have been in the cellar because of his transcendence rather than his immanence.

So the cellar diminished him yet again, in the same way as did the later reporting which often cited "tobacco heir" as his sole attribute, which did not adequately describe what he had done in his life. But that was what was in the paper, because he had been abducted not as a result of the books he had written but as a result of the magic sum which also floated through reports on him as an author or supposed allround Maecenas: three hundred million.

It would have been different if he had been able to do something just for himself and his own survival. He could do nothing, except that when he learned about the hand grenade he had the overwhelming sense of a duty not to allow his son to be orphaned. "You can, because you must," says Kant, and so at some point he developed the plan, which he himself knew to be unreal, of offering himself as a money courier to the kidnappers, a fairly desperate idea which had little chance of eliciting an ecstatic response from his captors. But he had the feeling that he had no right to discard a plan, any plan (if any were still feasible), for the sole reason that the predictable chances of its success were little better than nil. Nevertheless, these thoughts were occurring in something of an illusory realm and had almost nothing to do with that supposedly indestructible core of the personality that can withstand every external attack and underpin all resistance. On the contrary: as he was developing this plan, he wasn't sure if he was still thinking at all like a normal person, if an outsider would not tell him he had gone crazy a long time ago. This made him somewhat uneasy, but the unease took a backseat to everything else that was going on inside him. Perhaps, he thought to himself, I am actually going mad. So what? That would count if he were on the outside, and it was far from sure that he would ever leave the cellar again. The image of the core of a person had nothing to do with what he was experiencing. A much more accurate image was that of an empty space, and his feelings blowing through it. They came, they paused, they moved on, dissolved into others. There was no locus of resistance to act as a base from which to protect anything or keep it untouched.

With his thoughts, things were somewhat different. He could mostly, not always but mostly, think in an orderly fashion (even when he wasn't sure that he could manage it); most of all, he could avoid certain thoughts and ideas. He did not think all the way through the idea that his wife might have been killed by the hand grenade left in front of the house. He did not think about himself at home at all. He did go all the way to the brink: saw himself coming home, ringing the bell. His wife would open the door, call his son—then he had to break off his thoughts. He believed that if he thought himself into this scene, he would fall into an abyss of pain and misery out of which he might not reemerge. He put off sleep as long as he could, so as to be tired enough to avoid being exposed to the flights of thought that occur when sleep comes gradually. He also conjured up specific scenes which could be imagined exactly. A kind of path leading step by step into thought—in real time, as it were. Since one is usually moving too fast (not really advancing step by step, but flying over the route as if in a slow plane), he had to keep going back to the beginning again. Or he went on walks with particular friends, prepared classes for students, always working through a preset theme. If everything went well, sleep found its way into these thoughts and interrupted them.

A good means of distraction is naturally erotic fantasies, but I must admit that he could command these in the cellar only in the most limited way. On the one hand, he had set himself too many boundaries for the play of his thoughts, and on the other he had almost never indulged his fantasies in this kind of adventure. Even his dreams hardly ever concerned themselves with this aspect of his fantasy life. This too may demonstrate the difference between cellar and prison. It wasn't that *he* was lacking something, *he* wasn't there.

As for what concerned his body, it was merely an instrument that he had to keep in working order in case of his release, and his body took its revenge by no longer making an appearance (the mistake with the manic walking was his own, and the other exception was his headaches). The dualism—"he" on one side and "his body" on the other—was equally the fault of the cellar and persisted long after the cellar was over. Several weeks after his release, I was still having a frequent sensation that I was suddenly disappearing again, losing contact with the world around me. And sometimes the sensation was purely physical, only disturbing the surface of the body. I felt I would lose my mind if his/my body was not touched, taken in someone's arms, held tight, as if an external strength were required to save me from my own disappearance, and I needed to feel this strength against and on my body. It is also valid in this context that an internal reaction requires external criteria.

Consequently, one locates an inner "I" most easily in such effects of the division of self and body, of free-running thought and boundary-setting rule. But it is not simply "there" and it is not to be found just by looking. This "I" is itself a construct. The feeling that one "has" one is not the prerequisite for, but the result of, that construct's effects. During the first night, he had a remarkable experience. He had with much effort (being without his glasses) read the notice from the kidnappers and written out the answers to the questions about the addresses and phone numbers of his wife and trustees. He had not answered the question about the "caretaker" since there was no such person. He tried to sleep. Then it occurred to him that it might be a good idea to add a further explanation. They had probably been watching him and mistakenly identified someone as the caretaker. So he wrote down that there was a gardener who had retired six months previously, and a young successor. In both cases it would be pointless to turn to those people, because they would immediately notify his wife and his office and ask for instructions. When he had written these sentences, the shock, the fear, and the despair receded into the background. He felt almost euphoric. It was like a medicine suddenly taking effect, and yet it was due to nothing more than the fact that he had written a few sentences. Sentences which had not been dictated to him. He had contributed something to the situation. Broadened it, helped shape it. Taken the decision to provide a piece of information which could prevent the kidnappers from making mistakes that would cost time. However ridiculously small it seems, it allowed him to step out of total passivity and helplessness. It was not the fact that he had done something really important, but that he had done something at all, that was responsible for the sudden transformation in his mood. Stepping out of immanence. He had not found his "I," but had regained the feeling of being an "I."

He wrote every day. Not much, but regularly. Not messages to other people but a diary, in which he entered the thoughts and feelings that went through him. The diary did not allow him to engage and change his situation (even in fantasy), but he could make himself real. "It is already past 8 p.m., no one has come and I can hear nothing. Return of the anxiety that this could be the moment when they are going to leave me here. How long should I wait before knocking? When will I be certain that they're not coming? 8:30 p.m. Anxiety rising, worse than yesterday." It was sentences like these that made up the diary, very few reflections, and when they occurred, only in abbreviated snatches: "E. furious, police everywhere. What if E. is seeing ghosts? Is there any possibility of setting up situation which is immune to these fantasies? Not really. *Stop* thinking like this. Only causes panic." Next entries: "9 a.m. breakfast. (Cretin.) Washed. Slept till 11:30. No newspapers again (E. not here? Good sign, are they preparing something new?). 40 wall-ups. Any chance of news today? Hardly. Don't expect it." The anxiety did not diminish by the act of his writing it down. Nor was he using his writing to assure himself of a "core" that was untouched by the anxiety, because there was no such thing. Nothing remained untouched, he was the stopping place for anxiety. But the paper was a place that proved he could step outside himself. If one wants to look at it that way, the paper was the locus of his "I." He was literally accomplishing a transcendence.

He could not write the word "home." He did it once, and the results were terrible: he could no longer suppress what had to be suppressed from his thoughts. After that he just wrote "h."

Sometimes distance was impossible and writing became a kind of *écriture automatique*. Once he wrote out his son's and his wife's names in capital letters.

There were more than forty tightly written pages of interior monologue. (This too created problems of rationing and supply; he had to keep asking for paper and then for new ballpoint pens, because he kept using them up.) I wish I had his notes here, even though reading them would certainly be a risky business. These sediments of his feelings would allow me to build a bridge back across the space that separates me from them and only closes over again when his feelings suddenly displace mine and throw me violently out of the world again. He knew he would not be allowed to take the pages with him, although he sometimes hoped his kidnappers might agree after all. He was smart enough not to try to smuggle them out, although the desire to take them was overwhelming on the last day, for the Englishman searched him before leading him out of the cellar. The help it had been to him to write was linked to the pain caused by having to leave the results behind. He lost part of his personality in the cellar.

He also tried to write other thoughts. A kind of narrative which he had been planning for a long time. It got no further than an unplanned section which was the beginning of an analysis of Goya's *La Romería de San Isidro*. (Almost every day he had opened the book on the Prado to this great, calm, refined painting—a rapture of pure form in days of the most monstrous emotional chaos.) There were two sections which he decided on and could have written more or less without a library, and he began these but soon came to a stop. It was all so pointless. The themes of these essays belonged in the world, and he was no longer of it. It was more interesting and made the time pass much better to walk up and down, rather than write an essay on Christoph Martin Wieland's concept of the Enlightenment and another on a particular interpretation of the moral imperative. It was absurd. But what does "absurd" mean? The preparation of such essays had been part of his life (and hopefully would be again), and he had spent some of his happiest hours at the typewriter. But it didn't feel right anymore; the words wouldn't come, the thoughts didn't take shape, and the expectation that he could find a structure for them was nowhere to be found. He would like to have written essays, but he couldn't.

On the other hand, he was helped by the fact that he knew something about violent force and its consequences. Ironically, it had been his area of work at the Hamburg Institute for Social Research. He had read quite a lot about the effects of isolation, so some things did not surprise him. He did have light, but always the same light, or absolute darkness. Over a long stretch of time, absolute darkness is not dark. One sees lights, colored arcs, tiny sparks. The understimulated senses fill the sensory vacuum of their own accord. When the light was on, he sometimes saw something flash past out of the corner of his eye. When he switched off the light, he heard voices in the steady whir of the ventilator, distorted voices, as if being played back too slow. Or music. He might have been disturbed by this if he hadn't known it might happen.

What was bad was the knocking made by his guards to announce their arrival. Although he sometimes longed for it, it always gave him a fright. It signified power, and he understood it as such, and when you are powerless, any sign of power is always bad, even when you want to hear it, because it announces the only means of salvation. There was hardly a night when he didn't start more than once because he thought he heard the knocking. Sometimes he thought he was sure it was only in his head, but he never was entirely, so that he always positioned himself the way he had been ordered and called "*Ja! Yes! Come in!*" He had thought he would never again be free of this knocking, that he would hear it every night after his release. This was not the case. In the first weeks after he was freed, I never heard it at all, but then it did come sometimes, even louder than in the cellar, always like some ritual. One, two, three—accompanied by all its attendant phenomena: pounding heart, tensing of the body, fear. Since then, any actual knocking sound can give me quite a severe fright; a soft sound like a window shutter moving can jolt me out of the deepest sleep, make me wide awake and cold with fear.

This is neither surprising nor difficult to admit. Most people recognize something similar. ("From that day on, I've never been able to eat strawberry pudding"—big deal.) But something else has to be noted, because it belongs here and because it is what it is. In the story of the genie from the bottle in *The Thousand and One Nights,* the genie who has been released from the bottle says to his rescuer that, yes, he promised him all the treasures of the world for a thousand years—but now he wants to kill him. Since his time in the cellar, I can understand the genie, without really being able to make the story plausible. Fundamentally, what it's about is that from a certain moment on, it is impossible to continue rejoicing "properly" over your freedom. Your capacity to rejoice has been damaged. But that is only one side of things. The other is that you no longer feel you belong in the world into which you have been released, and the person who lets you out of the bottle or the cellar stands too close to you at his peril. It isn't that you want to take revenge. You just don't want all the baggage anymore, you don't want to carry that weight after your ability to bear it has been so damaged. This certainly will sound a bit too melodramatic. It was only thirty-three days of discomfort and anxiety. It was not years in solitary confinement, it was not torture, compared with what happens to people in the world every day.

And yet there was this understanding of the genie in the bottle, and more. I needed some time to admit it, even though I could feel it pressing on me. He had been visited more than once by this irrepressible longing, whether they allowed him to go home or not, to kill himself. He didn't go forward with it, but only because of a sense of duty to his family. He knew many cases of people who had suffered the worst physical and spiritual harm and then, after they had had some time to recover—or indeed years later—had killed themselves. He now understood these people quite well. There is only one guaranteed way to be sure you never go through THAT again, and that is quick, self-chosen death. Death seems easy compared with a life in which it is impossible to guarantee that THAT will not happen again. Even the fear that a so-called natural death (as if death were ever natural!) could just be a repetition of THAT, which means THAT would be awaiting you yet again, very quickly leads to its sequel, namely, to bring about the end yourself, thus retaining your autonomy.

On the twenty-fifth of March he was abducted; on the twenty-fourth of April the handover of the ransom was finally successful; during the night of the twenty-sixth of April he was set free. Less than a month later, the police found the cellar. Because the press was hot on the heels of the police, this could not be kept secret, even though it would have been extremely useful for the pursuit of the investigation. On the same day, I received a letter: an invitation on the occasion of the awarding of the Egon Erwin Kirsch Prize to give a lecture on "press reporting in general and with reference to your own case in particular," signed by a Dr. Funk on behalf of the publishers Grüner & Jahr, who recently, together with the Springer publishing operation, had acquired the photograph which my wife had banned from publication.

I watched the press conference on TV, tried to be pleased, urged myself to be happy that the police had found the cellar. I had been able to identify it beyond all doubt. The space in which he had been chained for thirty-three days was no longer somewhere outside the world, but was part of a house that you could look at and that had an address. They were searching for the perpetrators. Two of them had names and faces. And—it's a little embarrassing to admit it—it gave me satisfaction that after all the police talk about Mr. Reemtsma who only had to call for the kidnappers to have them come running to see what he wanted, and after the press articles whose writers perceived no cynicism in their use of the phrase "deluxe kidnapping," Michael Daleki, one of the police detectives, after visiting the cellar himself, admitted that he had some glimmer of an idea of what it might have been like to live chained up in it for almost five weeks. But still, I wasn't rejoicing.

And then there was still the letter from Dr. Funk. They had put him on display. They had done what my wife had tried to protect me from. Before, this hadn't mattered to me. Let them show his swollen, bloodied, beaten face. A document, nothing more. It was no longer me. But now I suddenly noticed the extent to which this effort to turn me into a public spectacle had hurt and repelled me, now when a second public spectacle was supposed to follow on the heels of the first. Before and After. And I was to provide the commentary myself.

And then it happened. From one minute to the next he was back in the cellar. The feeling was back again, smothering everything else or pushing it away. Nothing else was left. How can I describe it? A blend of paralysis, the extinction of all human spirit, the atrophy of all other emotions, like the lowest point of a depression that has been building for days, together with the tensing of every single nerve, an extreme, unstable agitation. A reprise of the combination of dulling despair and ceaseless impatient waiting. There had also been the fear of death in the cellar, a completely different feeling from the one just described, but so tied to it that you could have taken it for a consequence of fear, and he had done this at times, although he knew somehow and now was sure that these two feelings could not be reduced to a single entity.

The agitation grew along with the feeling of paralysis. I can't stand it any longer! was the only thought that could squeeze in. Then he began to walk. Three steps this way, three steps back. One, two, three, four, five, six, seven, eight, nine, ten, one hundred, two hundred, three hundred, four hundred—he was able to summon up the hope that nobody would come into the room and find him like this. Still better, he wished he were unconscious.

Does anyone understand me? His wife understood him. He heard the door, stopped pacing back and forth. He couldn't explain anything, he just hoped she would see that things were bad with him. She saw, and understood. He realized this as he began to weep helplessly, and finally, just as helplessly, said what he really wanted to say to each and every person in the whole world, so that they would finally pay attention: "It was so dreadful, so dreadful." But it didn't help.

His wife sat next to him with her hand on his shoulder. Why didn't she do more? Why didn't she help him? For a moment he felt like a child who isn't being properly comforted: Here, see what they did to me, and now I want a hug! She couldn't help him. She knew it, because she understood him, and he understood her, too. She knew the feeling herself. They knew that they could only sit next to each other, both isolated in their own feelings, but with a hand as bridge between them.

Nothing was over. Nothing would be over. The world could self-destruct again from one minute to the next. That is the truth that comes of thirty-three days. "You will enjoy your life ten times as much!" the Englishman had said, as if he wanted thanks for a cure for despondency and boredom. For this thoughtless piece of crudity, I hope he rots in jail. He did this to three people and I will hate him for it for as long as I have feelings.

It is not surprising that an experience like the thirty-three days in the cellar leaves the senses in many ways damaged. Agitation stamps each day; an unwillingness, almost an incapacity to wait for anything (it takes the utmost effort to maintain an everyday bearing); sudden noises trigger fear or an almost insane anger; the most ordinary things provoke the most extraordinary reactions, the slightest thing is an irritation. Your fellow creatures perceive this as "being strung out." It is tolerated, but not acceptable as a long-term condition. The strategy of appropriate behavior consists of demonstrating untroubled normality. This is recognized, indeed reckoned to be admirable. But soon what comes is the normality you have been striving for. And then? The habitual continuities resume, the extremes blur. You settle down. But sometimes, from one moment to the next, the totally other is back again and you are no longer of this world. Then, suddenly, the cellar is back in your life.

There are certain provocations, sometimes an accumulation of them, that unleash such an interior collapse. It was never a good thing for me to hear or to read anything about the kidnappers, or—see above—any "good news." But the effect of an article in the *Hamburger Morgenpost* was catastrophic; it was a speculation about the possible death of the criminal Thomas Drach. If he's dead, I thought, the others will fob everything off onto him, and the crime will never be fully solved. The person who gave the tip-off, the person or persons who acted as listening posts in Hamburg, etc., will never be named. There was a photo, too: Thomas Drach and girlfriend on vacation. I don't know how to describe it. First, the simple unwillingness even to look at it; stronger than any curiosity to know what the Englishman actually looked like. I felt mocked. It was a mockery that he was now on vacation enjoying his miserable life, a mockery that this man who by force of his own arbitrary assertion of power had become more important to me than any other human being, was on view with nice little pictures in the papers. That same stringer was earning his small heap of money with Drach photos, and the newspaper its bigger heap. And then by chance a letter arrived saying "Our joint conference next year cannot wait any longer." Cannot wait any longer. In the cellar: "I *cannot* wait any longer."

I had only skimmed the letter, which was absorbed into my bloodstream simultaneously with the photo in the newspaper. I started feeling worse with every day that went by, but without being ready to admit it. At some point I was on the telephone and suddenly had to struggle not to hang up on the person I was talking to. I tried to distract myself by reading the newspaper.

It was like being back in the cellar. He read words, was interested in nothing. He laid the newspaper aside, began to weep. Not convulsive sobs of despair. Just a few tears falling from his eyes. He sat there. Could do nothing else. Not even that very well. He pulled himself together, redirected his thoughts. The terrain of what was allowable was now a little larger. He wanted to have Drach's picture reproduced so that when he got into such moods he could shoot at it. Then he realized how soon this would become hackneyed. He imagined what he would do with Drach if the man fell into his hands, and lost himself in fantasies. Resurfaced somewhat sobered. And if someone brought me his head tomorrow, it would give me no satisfaction. And if I could do what I wanted without risk of punishment, what would I gain from undermining civilization in my turn? I want this man to answer before a court of law. I gain no compensation from hatred. The time in the cellar destroyed this symmetry, too.

Whoever has had something done to him wants revenge, and there is nothing contemptible about this. Sometimes revenge is therapeutic, sometimes not.

From the standpoint of civilization, revenge is not permissible, because if indulged, it would set off a dynamic of escalation which would soon run out of control. Crime requires punishment. First, because this is a deterrent. Second, to maintain the norms of what is prohibited, for a prohibition whose breaching is not followed by sanctions is nonexistent. (The theory of resocialization as the very rationale for punishment—rather than the way punishment is administered—is something I will not discuss here, because it is senseless and fundamentally barbaric.) What the *theory* of criminal law must not touch is the victim. Equally, punishment is extremely important to the victim. Not because it fulfills the requirements of revenge, because mostly it doesn't. But because punishment demonstrates the solidarity of the social group with the victim. Punishment shuts out the perpetrator and simultaneously embraces the victim. Punishment for the perpetrator is fundamentally the same as all the many friendly letters from people saying "Welcome back."

This greeting is of decisive importance for the resumption of one's emotional life. Despite the episodes I've just mentioned, I had enormous good luck. People made personal gestures and I received letters, for which I am more indebted than I am able to express here. But I have also realized (as have my wife and son) that the success or failure of such gestures develops its own criterion. A criterion that must prove itself against an extreme is always unfair, but that cannot be changed. The proverbial scales are always unfair because they weigh exactly. It is not always the right place or the right time to weigh things exactly, but somehow it is always unavoidable.

I admit that it is often difficult to distinguish hypersensitivity which has a specific cause from what is perhaps nothing but intolerance. In this connection, it may have been extremely stupid of me to be making the rounds of a scholarly conference a month after my release, but I wanted to get back as quickly as possible to everything I had been compelled to stop. As chance would have it, that was the day Thomas Drach was put on the wanted list. He now had a face and a name. He had last been seen in Cologne, his brother had been arrested there on suspicion of money laundering. The conference was taking place in Cologne, too. The press was already in force at the airport. They filmed me on the escalator, getting into a taxi, through the taxi window. "Why are you here, Mr. Reemtsma?" They were waiting for me in front of police headquarters, but I didn't show up. Later the newspapers reported I had visited a "private exhibition."

I enjoyed the conference and the participants. The conference recapitulated some of the irony of my situation: the last text I had finished writing before his abduction was about the concept of trauma, and the first conference I attended a month after his release was on the same theme. I also had the thought, or the hope, that I might find a professional context for my own situation here (the conference was being organized by the International Study Group for Trauma, Violence, and Genocide), an ambience that would support me if I could not live up to my own intention that I would carry on as if nothing had happened.

I was introduced by the psychologist who was opening the conference. But not only was the introduction oddly and excessively formal, it was also a document of the kind of emotional incompetence you would not expect from a psychoanalyst but (in my experience at least) would more commonly encounter outside the field of therapy in members of other professions. It also made a macabre point. He was especially pleased about the participation of Jan Philipp Reemtsma, and "that he is taking part despite everything he's been through. Because we couldn't assume that he would be able to come, we were no longer listing his name." (Or perhaps it was "we had taken his name off the list.") Such was the obituary for this particular member of the "Study Group." What he was referring to was the list of participants, on which they could certainly have continued listing me until they had proof I could not come. The use of the very word "list" with regard to a conference schedule which included first-person testimony of survivors of the Shoah is comment enough.

I don't want to go into the conference in detail. It and the participants both overtaxed me. Looking back, I see that it is simply not possible to have a discussion about the comparability of different etiologies of traumatization when there is someone at the table who was released from four and a half weeks as a hostage only a month ago. It is impossible to engage with the topic without this case becoming part of it, and such a conference cannot and could not have done so, even if I could. I should have been sufficiently discreet not to appear, for it is extremely hard to demonstrate that an utterly unrealistic expectation is warranted. It was interesting that I took all contributions to the discussion, particularly in an exchange about the comparable nature of different forms of traumatization, as referring to myself, interpreted them all as ways of talking that were meant to justify their avoidance of "my" theme. The egocentricity of a paranoiac functions in the same fashion. But sometimes paranoia is no more than what psychology describes as a perfectly adjusted perceptual attitude.

And then there are the dreams. Once I had a sequence of dreams, between which I woke up only to be dragged back leadenly into sleep, and I was dreaming historical scenes, or scenes that seemed to have something to do with history, in which I usually found myself in the role of the victim, and each time there was some kind of metaphorical bridge to his own experience. The dream was hyperdistinct in every one of its parts; there were no stand-ins as in so many dreams, I was physically present each time with every nerve intact. I awoke with the sensations still in my body and a sense of horror, as if I had actually lived through it all. Never, not even when I was a child, when I had some terrible recurring nightmares, have I ever dreamed anything approaching this in its dreadfulness.

A few weeks later I fell out of bed during the night. The dream I had been dreaming vanished instantaneously. All I knew was that there had been one, and that it had been terrible. I must have been hitting out in all directions, which had made me fall out of bed, and which may suggest that the dream had been about the attack itself. I went back to sleep. The next morning I felt as if I had lain awake all night; I could have gone to sleep at the breakfast table. My head was ringing, as if someone had hit it. How can I get through today quickly? I wondered. But then it will be night again. I realized it was the same feeling as in the cellar.

Fear of the day, fear of the night; only the hours stolen from the morning in sleep are bearable. Dreams like this come back frequently. Sometimes they transpose the feelings of anxiety and of being sent captive into another framework (concentration camp, death cell). The next morning I always have the feeling I have been awake all night; sometimes the shadow of the dream lies over the whole next day. Sometimes it is just the knocking—one, two, three—unconnected with a dream, that wakes me in the night. Once, in a hotel, I suddenly turned rigid with fear in my room. Didn't understand why. Then realized I had heard footsteps outside in the hall; I was waiting for the knocking, which didn't come.

And again and again, the sudden indifference to everything. Everything turning colorless. That's how it felt sometimes when he woke up during the night in the cellar, turned on the light, looked around: That's how it is. And perhaps I'll be here forever.

Somewhere in the Jewish tradition there is a description of what things will be like after the coming of the Messiah: everything will be the way it was, except fractionally displaced.

Not just since my abduction, I think that human utopias are human fears in distorted form. The feeling I have been trying to describe here can be summed up in almost no other way: everything is as it was, except it and I no longer quite fit together. As if I were wearing glasses that displace everything a fraction of an inch to the left or right. I can't get hold of things any more, the step no longer fits the stair. Or as if the surfaces of things were slightly curved, so that nothing that I set down would stand steady. World and self are no longer in harmony.

This can take on the form I have described of a combination of psychosomatic paralysis and extreme agitation, expressing itself in real physical pain. But it can also take the form of complete indifference. This is not the feeling that everything pales in importance compared with, say, an existential experience such as the confrontation with death. That's nonsense. It is not about something becoming unimportant by comparison with something else. It is not about feelings that can be transformed very easily into philosophical statements. Everything really has become unimportant, including the thought that everything has become unimportant. There is no trace in this of the emotion that is still preserved within depression and forms part of its etiology. The depressive founders against the world or in it. But when the world and I no longer fit together, then "becomes unimportant" means nothing that can be grounded in a particular feeling anymore, but reflects the straightforward fact that everything that is important is in the world, and only I am not.

That is how it is. The cellar remains in life yet cannot be made part of it. It remains the destructive irruption, the rape, the extraterritoriality, all of which can suddenly return. Occasionally there are moments when a kind of longing surges up in me for its capacity to reduce a situation to its essentials. When life seems too difficult and, compared with the difficulties, insufficiently rewarding, it sometimes happens that a wish forms to have a chain around the ankle again, to be in a very small room again that is utterly familiar in a way the world is not. Where does this atrocious wish come from? Simple. In the cellar, feelings of no-longer-being-part-of-the-world had their place. In the world itself, they have none. The only place I was at home with these feelings was in the cellar.

A Note About the Author

Jan Philipp Reemtsma was born in Germany in 1952. A philologist by training, he is the director of both the Hamburg Institute for Social Research and the Arno Schmidt Foundation. He lives in Hamburg.

A Note About the Translator

Carol Brown Janeway's translations include Bernhard Schlink's *The Reader,* Marie de Hennezel's *Intimate Death,* and Binjamin Wilkomirski's *Fragments: Memories of a Wartime Childhood.*

A Note on the Type

This book was set in Fairfield, the first typeface from the hand of the distinguished American artist and engraver Rudolph Ruzicka (1883–1978). In its structure Fairfield displays the sober and sane qualities of the master craftsman whose talent was long dedicated to clarity. It is this trait that accounts for the trim grace and vigor, the spirited design and sensitive balance, of this original typeface. Rudolph Ruzicka was born in Bohemia and came to America in 1894. He designed and illustrated many books, and was the creator of a considerable list of individual prints.

Composed by Stratford Publishing Services,
Brattleboro, Vermont
Printed and bound by R. R. Donnelley & Sons,
Harrisonburg, Virginia
Designed by Anthea Lingeman